"In the realm of leadership, there are countless books and thousands of theories. John Grinnell has separated fact from fiction. This book is about leadership principles that are tested and work, the rarest find. If you are interested in maximizing your potential and that of your management team and employees, this book is your roadmap. It will take you from where you are to where you want to be."
—Dan Davies, managing director, Executive Search, Vaco Raleigh, LLC

"I felt carried along a river of accumulating knowledge as I read *Beyond Belief*. John Grinnell has given us as good a guide for developing ourselves as leaders as any I've come across in many a year. Put simply, this book makes sense from start to finish. Bravo!"
—Tom Peters, author of the classic *In Search of Excellence* (rated the best business book of all time by the Bloomsbury Poll in Britain) and many other bestsellers and world-renowned management thinker

"*Beyond Belief* gives leaders at all levels of mastery a very rich concept for dramatically increasing their effectiveness and vitality. John Grinnell presents a leadership that is *beyond* the unconscious and self-limiting nature of our formative experience and current emotions. He relates this way of living and leading as a solution to problems within society, our government, our businesses, and our own minds and bodies. John has invested thirty years in learning and developing these insights and approaches, yet he presents them using current examples and metaphors. This book is an incredible gift to leaders and future leaders who want to plot a future with more choice, courage, and conviction."
—Jim Apple, chairman and CEO, First Citizens Bank

"If you are looking to lead your organization in a transformational way, John Grinnell has the blueprint for you in *Beyond Belief*. A must read for anyone wanting to grow an organization."
—Bill Clark, founder and managing partner, Clark Leadership Group

"John Grinnell pushes you to be more conscious of the choices you make so that you can break free of old patterns that are negatively affecting your business and personal lives."
—Jill Wells Heath, LEED® AP, president and CEO, Mulkey Engineers & Consultants

"Many leaders are guided by blind spots and false beliefs that both limit their personal potential as well as the success of their organizations. *Beyond Belief* gives leaders a map to escape these self imposed limitations."
—Jim McKelvie, chairman, Benecaid (Canada)

"Finally, a book that dares to deal specifically with today's leaders' biggest problem—themselves. Grinnell draws from decades of transformational work with hundreds of leaders to provide a proven and practical template for 'creating followership.' He advocates that people look honestly at the detrimental, habitual behaviors that deny them their best and most authentic selves as leaders. His approach focuses on self-awareness, ego, identifying negative behavioral patterns, choosing new behaviors, then 'riding the dragon' of emotional awareness so new and better outcomes are available for leaders and their followers."
—David B. Finch, president and CEO, ATCOM Business Technology Solutions

"There is a critical need for effective leadership and a fundamental lack in understanding of the defining elements of that leadership. Without strong organizational leadership to create an empowered decision-making environment the results typically are unaligned decisions, without accountability, and at best can only nudge an organization toward its goals. Creating an effective organization of empowered decision makers requires leading human behavior. Focusing on this leadership dimension is what makes John's book unique and an essential read for leaders as they face today's organizational challenges."
—Walt Yourstone, president, VT Milcom

Leadership Beyond Belief

Leadership Beyond Belief

Awaken Potential, Focus Leadership

Revised Edition of Beyond Belief

John Grinnell

Promethean-Mind Media
2019

Promethean-Mind Media
Chapel Hill, NC

www.grinnellmedia.com

ISBN 978-0-578-13101-6

Foreword

> Real leadership is . . . in effect, the adaptive force
> within an organization, creating the process that can
> change human perspective, thinking, and behavior.
> Rather than simply seeking a skilled analysis of com-
> petitive angles, it requires a commitment to act with-
> out the security of accepted behavior, to step beyond
> the usual boundaries in order to align the organiza-
> tion with its envisioned purpose and values.

So does Dr. John Grinnell describe the previously abstract concept of "Real Leadership" in *Beyond Belief: Awaken Potential, Focus Leadership.*

The Grinnell Organizational Vitality Model—Awareness, Align-ment, and Accountability—forms the fundamental basis for each of the five levels of leadership presented in *Beyond Belief.* It is the simplicity of this modeled approach toward educating for real leader-ship that makes it practical and easy to understand. The commit-ment, courage, integrity, and intestinal fortitude required in actually implementing the Organizational Vitality Model within an organiza-tion is where most of us struggle. As Dr. Grinnell unhesitatingly points out, we simply do not have the option—nor do we have the time—to struggle with committing, certainly not if we want to avoid slow death for the organizations and people we have both the honor and the responsibility to lead.

The case studies provided within the book validate critical con-cepts contained in the model, such as "on-purpose" thinking and the "One-Team" approach. Supported by figures and supplemental models, such as the Organizational Entropy and Comfort Zone Models, John illustrates the necessities of—and benefits provided through—expanded awareness within employees at all levels of a positive, functional organization. Additionally, I have found the appendices provided in the book to be convenient and useful tools to quickly refocus and reenergize when and as needed.

My firm, Grunley Construction Company, Inc., has actively worked with Grinnell Leadership for nearly a decade and has unquestionably benefited from their approach to enterprise-wide enhanced awareness. Initially, we agreed to send a half-dozen or so "Solid-State Leaders" to their one-week JumpStart program. The change we witnessed in those employees who were able to become aware, and hence, begin alignment with Grunley's mission and visions was quickly evident to me. Due to the positive results of the initial visit, we decided to send one member of our organization each month to attend the Jump Start program. Again, our organization benefited not only from those who attended and were on the path to awareness but also from those individuals who simply worked with the Grinnell graduates with their noticeable improvements in corporate culture and work output. John now spends one day per month at our headquarters providing ongoing analysis, feedback, and consultation to Grunley's entire executive team.

Even still, I must admit that it took me reading *Beyond Belief: Awaken Potential, Focus Leadership* to finally and fully comprehend how the Organizational Vitality Model—with all its interworkings—functions as a whole; for that reason alone, I am personally grateful to John for writing this book. More so, and perhaps more importantly, *Beyond Belief: Awaken Potential, Focus Leadership* reiterates the importance of developing real leaders ("We Need Leaders Now"!) in the face of the rapidly changing world around us and the uncertain future lying ahead.

Ken Grunley
CEO, Grunley Construction
Washington, D.C.

Contents

Contents

Introduction to the Revised Edition

Among the best organizations of all sizes and in any industry—there isn't much difference. Many egos would like to think there is, and we humans will fantasize and rationalize that there is, but in reality there isn't much if any. We can plug and play the best mangers from each of their companies into another with *no differentiation*.

Looking for answers, many are harping about "innovation" yet the reality is that technical and scientific systems innovations among competitors are roughly the same. Going to the same schools, reading the same journals, and going to the same seminars or working for numerous companies—most know what the others do. So technical or scientific distinction is not a big differentiator. Again, *no sustainable differentiation*.

The same can be said for your administrative systems, as most of your competitors use the same types of software. For example, in health care most of the major research and teaching hospitals we have worked with use the "Epic" system. In construction almost all use "construct-ware," and banking and so on are all very similar. Again, *no differentiation*.

Ironically, the only place there in fact can be lasting differentiation among comparable organizations is in the human system; yet most executives know much more about the other two systems, technical/scientific and administrative, than the one system that will actually allow them to compete more powerfully and *differentiate*.

Leadership Beyond Belief

The psychological-social (i.e., personal and cultural) underpin-nings of the human systems can be learned, but the result is an entirely new way of seeing, being, and doing. It has more to do with finding ways to unlock one's own, others', and the organization's potential than business planning, spreadsheets, or management systems. This new way can be illustrated in a model created by Jim Farr and refined in practice by Tim Gelbar,* the EOS/OAS/HS/LS model (figure 1).

Within our workshops at Grinnell Leadership, for more than twenty years now, I often ask the group, "What is a personality?" Few have gotten it right. I then point out how they know more about the details of the business they are in, or the car they drive, than the personality—the mechanism that will drive them through their life experience and to the level of success they can attain as leaders.

With the group now primed, I go on to the next question and ask them, "Which of the three systems is most important?" They then answer, "the human systems," and I point out they are wrong! All three systems are equally important. *If* you don't have excellent technology or administrative systems, it will hamper an excellent human systems. But a strong human system will often overcome a lot of the obstacles that a less powerful human system will be stumped by. The human system is the foundational system, yet the least understood because it is *intangible.* And that's the business I have been in for over thirty years, and the one my mentor the late Jim Farr, who was the first professional director at the Center for Crea-tive Leadership in Greensboro, NC, started almost fifty years ago.

You need to understand several important aspects of the human system if you are to learn how to work and lead effectively within it, and the book covers each, in separate chapters. I have developed another model to illustrate these aspects, the Grinnell Organizational

---

* Tim Gelbar is a longtime client and friend; we both learned a great deal from Jim Farr, PhD. The perspective about "how to differentiate" was further developed by Tim Gelbar as he led AMEC Power and Process Americas from a $200 million per year design-build firm to one with a $2 billion backlog—with industry-beating EBITA. He used a "human systems" approach like the one found in this book and thereby proved, as many others have, its validity within the real fire of production.

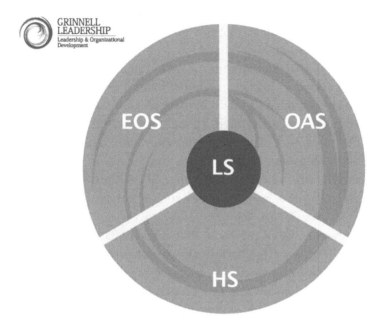

Figure 1. The EOS/OAS/HS/LS Model. EOS = Expertise operating system; OAS = Organizational administrative system; HS = Human system; LS = Leadership system.

Vitality Model (see figure 2 in chapter 1). The first step is staying on purpose, and keeping yourself, your followers, and your organization focused on that purpose. In doing so, you must act accountably—both you and your followers must be held accountable to the goals set for fulfilling the purpose. To achieve those goals, the leader must seek alignment of behavior of all those working to achieve the goals, first their own. And undergirding all these steps is awareness, of self and others. Putting all these components together enables effective leaders to transform organizations and help them reach the goals that fulfill their envisioned purpose. When you understand these aspects of the human system and how they relate to effective leader-ship, you will have begun to learn to leverage the human system—and how to lead within it. You will be on your way to leading beyond belief through existing boundaries. Yet there are more two more important and fundamental aspects to leading the human system. Simply stated but not simplistic in application, they are self-awareness and its partner courage.

You will discover through the many examples of leadership failure and success provided in this book that all organizations are based on the individual with all their thoughts, feelings, decisions, and actions. The most powerful aspect of leadership is the individual and their self-awareness and courage to operate outside of the dictates of their personality and ego to be more aligned with a purpose whereby they heighten the probability of personal, familial, and organizational success.

As you read through the book, reflect on the successes and maybe even more importantly the failures you and those who you have worked and lived with over the years have experienced. In doing so remember that not one of them intended to fail. No one drove to work each day writing down what they should do to not be successful. Doing the best they could, it was a lack of self-awareness or courage and hidden beliefs that subsequently drove their off-purpose behavior and action that snuck up and sabotaged their success. Self-awareness is not a guarantee of success, but it sure does prevent many of our unintendedly off-purpose unintended negative outcomes in our lives and leadership.

Chapter 1
We Need Leaders Now
Awaken Leadership

Early one morning a few years ago, just before dawn, I prepared my boat for a trip with my friend Chris Conway out to a reef called the "Red and White" about thirty-five miles off the coast of North Carolina to fish for grouper. It was a beautiful, calm morning with the morning glow of the eastern sky lighting the horizon and the gentle breeze carrying the smell of salt water and marsh, and softly rattling the outriggers of the boat. I completed my safety checks and barely bumped the throttles, maneuvering the boat away from the slip. A touch of adrenalin flowed, as it always does when I head offshore. Still, it was a calm day with no hint of stormy weather in the sky.

With twin engines humming their synchronized tune and the sun just peeking over the Masonboro Island between us and the ocean, we cruised a mile north to the Carolina Beach inlet. It's a well-dredged natural inlet without jetties, and can be a little treacherous for boaters, but those of us who navigate it regularly know to stay between the buoys; if you do, you will be safe, even in rough water. At least, that had always been the guideline. The week before, however, a nor'easter had hit the inlet and significantly altered the sand shoals within it. I had been traveling for two weeks and did not know about the storm.

Leadership Beyond Belief

As we turned into the inlet, I pressed the throttles forward and the adventure further as we headed out the inlet. As we cruised, we noticed sizable surf breaking in the middle of the well-marked channel between the buoys. It wasn't supposed to be there. Once you're in an inlet like that, the last thing you want to do is turn around into a three-knot tidal current pushing you toward the ocean. I began to feel fear; adrenaline flowed, and my focus became acute. My mind told me, "Stay inside the buoys!" I realized, though, that if I stayed in that course that had always been the safe way to go, we would likely run aground, which could destroy the boat, and injure my passenger and me. The course through the inlet that had always been the safe one was now dangerous—*conditions had changed*. Chris told me to read the water, forget the buoys, and alter my usual course by veering into deeper water. My rational mind told me he was right. But when I thought about changing course, a strong gut feeling surged through me, a fear of the unknown, and a voice inside urged me to stay the course between the buoys. But I *consciously* chose to do as he counseled and left the comfort of my past ways. I went against my "gut" and we made it through the inlet without mishap. I chose to listen and incorporate Chris's input and deliberately changed course to address changed conditions.

Must Know the Box to Get Out of the Box

Leaders face similar situations often, usually not so dramatically physical, but with serious consequences if they make the wrong choice. If they choose what seems the safe channel through churning waters, the course they've always followed, they're exercising leadership, in a sense—"indecision making," in other words. Leadership of some sort is inevitable, but the question is whether it is effective leadership. As noted in chapter 5, the non-action resulting from indecision making reflects a decision, but it does not reflect real leadership.

We typically follow the safe, habitual way of acting individually or in an organization because of our beliefs. When we hear "belief," we tend to think of religious views or philosophical outlook on life, but "belief" has a broader meaning; beliefs, in fact, shape *all* of our perceptions, decisions, actions, and outcomes. "Belief" has a specific meaning in the context of leadership, behavior, and awareness: beliefs are theories based on past data. We usually act based on what we believe about a situation. We were not born with these beliefs, we developed them—and they're not irrational. Indeed, beliefs and the automated behavior that springs from them are essential for ordinary daily life and for survival. Imagine if you had to stop to think about how you were going to walk or eat or pronounce words. You would waste so much time and energy that you wouldn't have any capacity left for analyzing a situation, driving a car, or acting quickly enough in a life-threatening crisis to survive.

The problem with beliefs is that because they're part of a survival mechanism in our minds, and because they're our theories about reality in our minds, they become ingrained, and they lead us to act habitually. Once they become well formed, they also lead us to react emotionally when new experiences challenge them. Emotional reactions are powerful, and difficult to control. Because they're based on belief—theories built on past data—they may not be relevant and may not provide an optimal response within a new situation. Beliefs can guide us, but they won't enable us to make better judgments or change direction in critical and unique situations. My inner voice's telling me to stay the course in guiding my boat arose from unconscious belief, formed by many fishing trips through the inlet. That theory based on past data led me to see danger in changing course. But the theory was now unsound and outdated; conditions had changed. My inner voice was wrong. I had to override that old belief and go against my gut feeling if I was to navigate the inlet successfully. I had to move away from emotion-based leadership.

Self-awareness, on both personal and organizational levels, enables us to recognize the beliefs of an organization and individuals within it—including, first of all, ourselves. When we are not aware of our beliefs, they run the show instead of us. Beliefs are like the hidden wires behind walls that power our lights. They operate beneath the surface of consciousness, manifesting in our perceptions, judgments, decisions, and behavior as leaders. The degree to which a leader or leadership team running an organization is unaware of the beliefs that drive their decision making and behavior is the degree to which they are out of control of the situation that confronts them *now*. When they are out of control in this way, they are letting themselves be led by automated, noncreative behavior based on old data lead—behavior that may run them aground.

In this light, the problem is that we call people leaders when they are not. They then think they are leading when they can't. Most can't because they don't really understand what leadership is, are blinded by their ego's fear, or are unwilling because they don't have the stomach for it. Leadership can be learned, but just because a person is a boss or can charismatically stand up in front of a crowd doesn't mean that person can lead.

Knowing versus Doing Leadership

Knowing what to do and doing it are two very different things. By example, a very experienced manager/leader I worked with years ago illustrates the difference. I remember him sitting across from me—sixty-two years old and scratching his head in thoughtful frustration, the founder of a company was at the end of his rope. He had tried for years to transition the company to someone who could pick up the ball and run with it. It hadn't happened yet and he now doubted whether it ever would. The financial transition incentives were well thought out, but that had been clear for years. He got anxious every time he thought about being saddled with the daily grind of continued operational responsibility. Not to mention he wanted to spend more time with his wife traveling as they had always planned yet postponed year after year. As he spoke the sadness was almost palpable. Having started the company forty years ago just out of school, he told me it had been a great ride. Only in the past few years had he lost some of the fire. Unlike his previous attempts to transition (which were many), I could sense he was ready to move on now, but another quandary was his current employees. Many had loyally followed him for years and were a few years younger, in their fifties; he worried what would happen to them if the company was acquired, and he said that solution was off the table. The larger concern for him was that he

8

didn't know how to pass on the company spirit or "soul"—that fire in his belly—to the next generation. As we sat there his appearance began to shift. Clearly he was thinking deeply about something, and I asked him what was going on. He looked up and said, "for the first time I have been thinking lately I may be the problem." Before then he had always placed the leadership problem of succession and the sustainability of the enterprise outside himself.

As he talked I began to see the rationalizations he had used in the past to protect himself from initiating change. Always seeming rational, they are hard to spot. At times he may have had the wrong person, or operations were amidst a big change, or market timing was not right. The difference this time is that he looked within and openly admitted that he may have been the problem all along. Not until he accepted responsibility for the effects of his leadership—or the lack thereof—would things really change.

It's always that way; surrendering ego (which never wants to be wrong) is simple to say yet hard to do. Real leadership, the type that makes a real difference, "that is a difference," is rare and always based on a personal decision and full commitment to leave the certainty and comfort of past approaches, misaligned beliefs, and ego comfort. He had the capability all along; the challenge he fought was never outside himself, but rather inside—the place where real leadership starts. There was no guarantee of success—there never is. But he had taken that first and most difficult step as a leader—to lead oneself.

Once the commitment was made, it took about eighteen months for a full transition. He set up a year-long in-house leadership development process that rebuilt the network of relationships to support a younger president and the senior staff. He taught many of the sessions himself, passing on knowledge, not technical, but stories that conveyed the defining moments that shaped the character of the company—he talked about leadership. He shared memories about the start-up of the company and the excitement and fear therein. He talked about the fast-growth phase and its challenges. He and his senior executives discussed in great detail how decisions were made. They held dialogue about times when they followed their company's core values and purpose and thereby thoughtfully chose to "do the right thing" instead of taking the easier path that seemed logical, full of common sense and financially rational. He and his senior staff engaged the younger leaders in meaningful conversations about their customers and vendors over the years—the good ones and the tough ones. In essence, he focused the year-long program on the moments of real leadership decision, action, and consequence. The leaders were initiated into the soul of the company. He had successfully passed the torch and more importantly *preserved the flame.*

The founder finally retired and spent a couple of years traveling with his wife. They still love to travel, but a few years ago he started another business, which is smaller and takes less of his time. He is very successful in his new venture and he and his family are happy and enjoying their new lifestyle.

Real leadership is one of the most rewarding but difficult challenges a human being can undertake. To step up and do what others can't do or will not do is why there are so few real leaders. Most don't have the stomach for it. It starts from within oneself and moves out to others. It has less to do with intelligence and analytical ability and everything to do with perspective, integrity, and courage.

Leadership Failure

Failure of leadership and the consequences of that failure are all around us. Think back over the past decade or so: the Enron debacle, leading to the Sarbanes-Oxley legislation and requiring time, energy, and financial resources that could have been spent elsewhere, but instead was used to provide regulations to control the few cheaters. And then there was the mortgage crisis. It began with good intentions on the part of many—enabling all Americans to own houses and get ahead—but led to devastating consequences we are still experiencing. More recently, we've seen the IRS appearing to target certain populations in our country. Venture capitalists make a good living buying low and selling high as they find failing, poorly led companies— buying them for pennies on the dollar. Much of the effort to build those companies from an idea to their pinnacle was lost. As these scenarios unfold we see people hiding, pointing the finger, blaming others and circumstance, resulting in chaos, with most not seeking responsibility (as the founder did). And again, little is learned, with history repeating itself over and over again. Many have given up hope, believing with grim resignation that we will never be able to escape the gravitational pull of human nature and unaware leadership. I don't believe this is true, but these failures do represent the next major challenge in the evolution of leadership. That is, to awaken and learn to look within with awareness to become more effective. The examples of failed leadership above are just the tip of the iceberg, the issues the media points our attention toward.

Think about the myriad decisions made daily in our businesses and local governments, and their effects. According to a 2010 McKinsey report by Clay Deutsch and Andy West, up to 75 percent of mergers and acquisitions don't work out the way they were intended to. As we all know, this often results in a financial loss, but also a huge loss of talent and value plundered by competitors and head hunters. Frequently an essentially well thought out strategy to migrate a business to a more sustainable future is not led well and thereby is overly resisted by the very people who will one day lose their jobs because of a loss of market share due to an inability to change fast enough. We see successful executives with no energy left for the families they love on the weekends, leading to divorce, and alienation from their spouses and children, or an unnecessary loss of personal health. And none of these outcomes were intended or wanted, and the good news is that they are completely unnecessary.

Good People, Bad Habits

The aforementioned public, business, and personal crises, broadly publicized or not, I believe, were created by good people gone wrong—good people with the wrong habits driven by beliefs and mind-sets they were unaware of or failed to recognize and underestimated the outcomes their actions created. The premise of this book is that if the persons making the decisions that led to those outcomes had understood how human nature operated, had understood the mind and behavior and themselves, they could have gained necessary perspective and made different choices. I doubt if any of them were aware of what led them to the place where they (and we) ended up. What these crises have in common is the failure of those directing the organizations to see clearly and truly lead themselves.

The Basis of Leadership: Self-Knowledge

Perhaps paradoxically, leading with full potential and meaning begins with self-knowledge. It has more to do with our beliefs, relationships, ways of communication, and actions than the content of what we say. It is in large part an ability to reach a clear and balanced perspective, and align purposeful action with an envisioned future. It is being at choice and not reflexive. It is becoming aware and as a result awakening to that central and often hidden conscious self that can operate most effectively toward these ends. A colleague years ago, Anthony Speed, Ph.D., called this often hidden self the "leader-self." Another colleague, Jim Porto, Ph.D., at the University of North Carolina at Chapel Hill, calls this process of growing awareness "self-leadership." This kind of leadership involves developing a consciousness that can see beyond the limitations of past belief, decisions, and experience; it is taking action courageously.

Fundamentally this book is about giving you the perspective and skill to reach more of your hidden potential and aligning that potential with others to achieve common goals. In making visible how to reach your potential as a leader, the perspective found in this book, if taken to heart, can help to release the chains of past practice and perspective and help you find the way to greater satisfaction and happiness in your life while achieving success professionally.

This concept of becoming aware of hidden potential is abstract. More concrete types of thinkers want metrics and tests, and can have trouble grasping the abstract. It is easier, after all, to understand a manufacturing or banking operation or monthly sales goals than such abstract concepts, because those operations are concrete and measurable.

We Need Leaders Now

Most experienced leaders know that they are leading human behavior. Yet the most enlightened, if they are leading at the differentiating leverage point, lead human minds. More specifically, they must lead the beliefs that run those minds.

The mind is an abstraction. The mind prompts people's perceptions, reactions, and behavior, which are what cause the results in organizational life. By knowing how to *use* this insight, leaders can consciously create conditions that allow people's motivations and personal potentials to be directed toward a chosen, better outcome. Without this insight, leadership is largely hit or miss, is often frustrating, and generally reverts to "telling" or "pushing" followers, which in most cases proves to achieve suboptimal results. If you want to lead at the leverage point, you must learn to see then work effectively with the abstraction of human belief. The point of this book.

At their own peril some executives will dismiss a psychological approach as "touchy-feely" psychobabble.

Thirty years ago, as a young twenty-something-year-old entrepreneur with a small construction company to help pay for my doctoral education, I attended my first leadership seminar, which was presented by the late Dr. James N. Farr. At that time I struggled with the concepts presented in this book as I became frustrated with the abstractions and psychological theory Jim presented. At one point, I told him, "Just give me a set of plans and a crew, and at the end of the day I can put it behind me." Jim looked over his glasses at me and asked, "What makes you think human beings are any less understandable and predictable than reading blueprints and building a building?" He went on to add, "For you to find your potential, you must understand what drives your personality and its behavior, perceptions, and actions, and then make a choice to act differently to create what you want." At the time I thought it hogwash. Now I know differently.

13

Leadership Beyond Belief

After more than three decades of applying the behavioral sciences to leaders and organizations, I can say he was right. Humans are, in fact, rather predictable. When you pull away the façades we erect, we are amazingly similar, but grasping this point requires a different way of seeing. Being a successful leader of an organization involves knowing about people more than anything else. Many business executives, though, tend to dismiss a psychological approach, seeing it as merely "touchy feely" psychobabble. To be most effective and reach their potential, however, leaders must be able to understand themselves, predict their own behavior, and better control themselves to be able to create outcomes through the effort of others. To do this requires in-depth knowledge of human nature—and intent to understand oneself.

The Grinnell Organizational Vitality Model

A model is *not* truth. It is a lens to look through to help a leader see with new eyes that can then chart a path for greater success. One model has helped thousands when put to use. The model consists of four success drivers and an action catalyst. The drivers are: Expand Awareness, Seek Alignment, Act Accountably, and Be on Purpose. The *catalyst* is called the "Leadership Leap" and makes the model come to life with action for real breakthrough. A chapter in this book is devoted to each element, but a high-level explanation follows here.

Expanding Awareness—of both self and secondarily of others—is the foundation of *all* leadership. It is used to initiate the process of finding greater hidden potential. It is the foundation of finding new and better ways and options for success. Erik Erikson, a famous psychologist, used to say, "The person with the most options wins [in life]." I like to say, "The leaders with the most options wins." The ability/skill to generate perspective "at will" can be learned and is the first essential step for breaking free of past experiences, habits, and rote patterns of perception, thinking, and behavior to chart a course that meets the future more effectively. It is challenging in that perspective is needed when the ego with its defense mechanisms fights to preserve the familiar at all cost. Knowing where you are headed (purposefulness) transforms this fear into creative tension (Senge 1989).

14

Figure 2. The Grinnell Organizational Vitality Model

Being on Purpose can be called focus. That is knowing what you want to experience in the future. It can be personal, familial, organizational, or social: it is the future the leader is creating through his or her On-Purpose decisions and actions. This together with the other elements of Seeking Alignment with others and Acting Accountably form what I call the Grinnell Organizational Vitality Model (figure 2) or also the Angel Model (which I'll explain later).

Once greater perspective is gained through expanded awareness, the second area, **Seek Alignment**, fosters sometimes difficult discussions for understanding and mutual cooperation in aligning decision making and action with others. Operating in alignment with the values, mission, and team implies "integrity," whereas we often find hypocrisy used out of fear of alienation in an excessive drive for advocacy—saying one thing in the meeting to the boss and another to a more trusted colleague. True alignment is always judged with the larger purpose and intent of the organization, its customers, and its employees and so on. There can be compromise and trade-offs, but only after the often avoided difficult honest discussion to find real clarity around the intended and unintended impacts of decisions.

The next success driver, **Acting Accountably**, requires courage and is often compromised for the wrong reason. Acting accountably ensures that the leader, the organization, teammates, and followers will carry out the actions necessary to reach the purpose, even though those actions may run counter to the longtime, habitual behavior of the organization and those within it. This aspect of leadership often breaks down as people either do not know how to do it or feel they don't have permission to do it, or can't seem to get beyond a sometimes real but often imagined risk of a damaged relationship and reputation. When compromise is done for the wrong, often fear-based reasons, it throws others and the organization and its purpose under the bus for emotional comfort's sake.

The Catalytic Leadership Leap

Catalytic to the leadership process is courage, because changing habitual behavior often arouses fear in self and others. Just like the retiring business founder I used as an example earlier in this chapter, many leaders know what they ought to do to achieve an envisioned goal, but often they can't make the required jump across an imagined emotional barrier. Instead, they retreat to the seemingly safe traditional ways of operating in the organization, even when following those ways of the past may create disastrous consequences. This emotional barrier to taking the right action is located in what I call the "Sea of Uncertainty" or the "Quit Zone." Seeing clearly what the organization, family, or self needs to do and where it needs to go is the first step, doing it is the second more difficult one. That is why leaders often confuse planning with action as an emotional hedge. Developing the courage to take self first and then followers in a new direction requires the leader to withstand the pressures of uncertainty and possible alienation.

Chapter 2
Being On-Purpose

"Doc, what do you think my purpose is?"
"Look around. It's the life you are living and the performance of your organization now."

Imagine you are standing in a dark room. You can't see anything except a three-foot circle on the wall from the projected light of your flashlight. It has some words written in it, including names of people, places, and dates. There are thousands of other three-foot circles you could project onto the wall, containing different words describing alternate experiences, but the only one you see is the one you are pointing your flashlight at, and so it is the only one you know about and get to experience.

You've been pointing at this three-foot circle for most of your life. In fact, it is your life. I could have filled in a different circle. I could be an offshore fisherman with hair down to my ass. But instead, I work as a behavioral scientist in leadership and organizational development. I am the father of three with a wonderful wife, and I do, in fact, like offshore fishing with friends. Within my three-foot circle, I am in familiar territory. For most of my life, I have been unaware of the other thousands of three-foot circles that exist in the darkened room. Since I don't know they exist, I certainly won't experience them. Organizations are the same!

Yet sometimes I get a feeling that I want to do something else, but then—why, I can't really explain—the sense that it's important to

keep my flashlight aimed where it is on the wall rises in me powerfully, sometimes even when my organization, happiness, marriage, or
health is taking a beating within that circle. This is normal human
behavior, but real leaders have to be abnormal.

I have embellished it a good bit over the years, but I remember
when I was first told the flashlight analogy by my friend and mentor
the late James N. Farr, Ph.D., while studying a martial art called
Aikido together in the early 1980s when I was in my late twenties. It
awakened me to the fact that what we see and experience is a direct
reflection of what we believe to be true about ourselves, others, our
potential, and life possibilities.

As an example of someone with a different flashlight and circle
than me, my cousin is a brilliant businessman in the Washington,
DC, area. As a young man he got into real estate, and he has done
very well. Years ago he wanted a beachfront home in Rehoboth
Beach, Delaware. He took what I perceived to be a big risk and
bought a number of side-by-side oceanfront lots. I thought he might
end up stuck with them and take a hit financially. But he soon
enough sold a few lots, which paid for his house. In other words, his
flashlight pointed to a spot on the wall that allowed him to see things
from an angle I didn't see in my circle. He got a free house. The option
of doing what he did was outside my three-foot circle and, therefore,
my leadership. But he knew his purpose from the beginning: to get a
house at little or no cost. With that purpose in mind, he knew how to
be what I call "on-purpose." He probably didn't have a clear plan in
mind when he started, just a concept, but it was a purpose. He had a
target and he had the courage to aim at it and follow through. He had
the courage to jump. No wonder he has done so well over the years.

Leadership Is Abnormal

A couple of years ago, I facilitated a strategic planning retreat with a
client in the banking industry. As we all know, it is going through a
tumultuous time, fraught with change. The CEO passed out a really
good article about how important it is to change in order to successfully address the fast-approaching future in the financial industry,

but how banking culture finds change difficult. The article kept referring to the "new normal." Soon all the executives starting using the term "new normal," which aligned with the message in the article and the usual type of strategic thinking.

Something about this bothered me. After some reflection, I realized what it was: the bankers were looking for "certainty" again. So I said to the group, "Aren't you looking to find the 'new abnormal?'" It stopped them cold. Now, I have been working with this team for years, and these executives are rather advanced in their leadership abilities, but even after all these years they were again hypnotizing themselves back into finding certainty instead of seeking the right future. Regardless of what they came up with at the retreat, they were automatically following their unconscious purpose of "feeling certain" instead of "being on-purpose."

And that is the essence of what leaders do. They create the "new abnormal." They point their flashlights toward different spots on the wall and new, more appropriate targets. They don't make their target the one that accompanies their feeling of certainty. This is also why people don't usually like real leadership at first, as it creates feelings of uncertainty. But it also is their ship bound for the future.

Uncertainty is not a good feeling for people just beginning on the path of true leadership. Yet the mature transformational leader knows that when uncertainty is linked to purpose, it is what Peter Senge, in his wonderful book *The Fifth Discipline* (1990), calls "creative tension." Uncertainty alone, without a clear and right target aligned with the better future you want to experience, gives you only anxiety. With a target, a leader knows how to *be on-purpose*, creative tension kicks in, and the pain of uncertainty becomes the elixir of organizational vitality. Being on-purpose is the bet against organizational entropy, what Robert Quinn, in his book *Deep Change,* calls "slow death." But as a leader, you have to remember that most normal human beings want to keep pointing their flashlight at the same three-foot circle because of their unconscious desire for "certainty" and for staying "normal." It's your task to get them to see the abnormal and the often unreasonable, to aim the flashlight at a different circle, and your challenge is to keep them watching that new circle as you lead them into the unknown future.

Clarifying and Focusing

Without purpose, human beings do not have a sight on their gun. They do not know how to aim their decisions and leadership behavior. They don't know when they are off-purpose. With a clear purpose, a leader has a sight and can assess and analyze the current conditions of his or her life, leadership, and organization. Leaders can see the gaps between where they are and where they need to be. They and others can take "on-purpose" action.

A model of using purpose to enable you to see the gaps (see figure 6 in chapter 4) was introduced clearly to me by one of the most strategically minded leaders I have met in my career, John Tarpey. Tarpey explained that with a clear intent, a purpose, leaders can see what is "at gap," or out of alignment with the target. They then go about with purpose, changing those aspects of the organization, including their behavior and that of their followers, technologies, infrastructure, and people that stand out in stark relief. To foster change, a purposeful leader turns the gaps into objectives and plans how to meet those objectives. We might call it "closing the gaps." Again, certainty is not the guide; doing the right things is.

On-Purpose Leadership

Every employee impacts the mission in some way. The exceptional leader does not put himself between followers and the organizational purpose/mission and values. He or she steps aside and points the way; helping others understand the outcome that they impact, the leader then encourages and helps followers align with the outcome, not the leader. When employees are out of alignment the exceptional leader provides direct, timely, and respectful input and feedback that the purpose is "on purpose" or "off purpose." This approach stands in stark relief to the leader who stands out front and thinks the purpose and values are his or hers. This subtle yet profound shift in perspective and leadership behavior reduces ego resistance to change and moves people into a state of responsibility for their performance. *This*

Leadership Beyond Belief
is not a play on words but rather a profoundly powerful approach that is the basis for empowering others! Language matters.

On-Purpose Beliefs

The most obvious aspect of alignment with purpose is being on-purpose with our behavior. This has to start with being on-purpose with our mind. All outward behavior is driven by the mind and its beliefs, so all real transformation starts with a shift of mind. Mastering our mind and its beliefs is one of the biggest challenges in life— and one of the most rewarding. Most of us don't even realize that the mind is not who we really are; so we continue to believe it when it tells us the same thing over and over, when it feeds us habitual beliefs that can often keep us from being on-purpose.

During the past downturn in the U.S. economy the president of one company, a brilliant manager who has almost singlehandedly, under the overall leadership of the CEO, led their company to phenomenal growth, met with the CEO. The president referred to the poor economic outlook and worried that the company might be spiraling deeper into a depressive hole. After he had spoken for a while, the CEO interrupted and said, "We must continue to believe there is a market for our services." He was right. If there is no belief in the value of the service, then why even have a business and strive for excellence? The real leader has the ability to hold the organization to its purpose and to manage his or her mind to be on-purpose when others can't or won't. This is not denial, as real leaders are also always curious about the current reality as it relates to purpose.

Holding followers to the purpose does not mean being punitive; it means being conscious of human nature, and how most people typically operate under habitual beliefs and behavior. Being conscious in this way, on the other hand, does not imply *not* holding people accountable. It does imply that staying on purpose in changing times requires changing minds. People in the organization must come to believe that "we will find a way to make our service viable in our market or we will find a new market where we can flourish." The real

22

leader must plant in followers that new belief and illuminate for them the purpose that will make it true.

In this regard I think about the changes IBM has made in the almost three decades I have been consulting. The company has moved from being Big Blue and dominating the manufacture of mainframe computers to being a consulting group as personal computers took hold in the market to now putting in and supporting the information systems of the world as the market changes yet again. When I see IBM, even though I have never consulted there, I know that culture cultivates transformational leaders. They know how to close the gap.

Being On-Purpose with Behavior

When a leader decides to interrupt the automated routines of habit to create a different future, if a true transformational change is to occur—one that will make the company more competitive and more satisfying for the people who work there—the leader and his or her followers must behave in new ways. The key to this new behavior is being on-purpose.

Without purpose, human beings are left with only their memory-based beliefs, habits, and experience to dictate how they perceive and respond to current and future conditions. Without purpose and clearly ranked values, people are unable to escape from this automatic loop of perceiving and responding out of reflex in the same ways they always have. Armed with clarity of values and purpose, individuals throughout the organization can judge for themselves right from wrong (on-purpose from off-purpose), which empowers. The new behavior required for transformation to a satisfying future grows out of awareness of purpose tied to self-awareness, which chapter 7 describes.

Without purpose, even if people are aware that they need to act differently to achieve a better outcome, they will most likely continue on the same course, choosing the comfort of past behavior over the emotional challenge of venturing into uncertainty. They experience anxiety, but not creative tension, because they are not self-aware.

23

Leadership Beyond Belief

This anxiety is why breaking the inertia of habitual action is hard for most people.

Off-purpose behavior in an organization has a cascading effect; it leads to poor relationships and team dynamics, which lead to bottlenecks of information flow, which reduce a leader's ability to use good analytical and decision-making skills, which results in poor planning and execution. The ultimate result is failure to achieve goals and sometimes failure of the organization itself.

Since I'm a fisherman, I like to use an analogy to the charter fishing business to illustrate for organizations the outcome off-purpose behavior can lead to, a "fishing story," if you will:

There was once an experienced charter boat captain who was bright and capable, with years of experience running his boat and operating his charter business. Times became tough, though, and his business suffered like the rest: the number of customers dropped over several years. As the economy began to pick back up, he decided he could accommodate more customers than he typically had on a trip. In case of an accident at sea, though, the boat would need a larger life raft to hold the additional passengers. He calculated the risk of accident versus the cost of a new raft. He and the other charter captains he knew had sailed these waters for years without mishap. The captain did not seek counsel from an outside, unbiased source. He gave the most weight to how much his company would earn this quarter. He decided not to spend the money for a larger life raft.

Unfortunately, he had miscalculated the risk. Changing weather patterns and currents brought some unexpected conditions, and his boat hit a shoal a good distance offshore. Now, treading in the frigid blue water along with his mate and several passengers, he agonized over the wrong decision he had made. The captain, like all too many leaders today, had analyzed the situation but hadn't correctly emphasized the social responsibility he bore in his decisions and leadership. If he had taken time to set out his purpose, he could have come up with a purpose such as "provide an enjoyable fishing trip for customers in which they and the crew sail safely and return safely to port." The safety of his passengers and crew should have been paramount, but he didn't stop to set out a purpose, which not only would lead to a satisfying outcome for everyone but also would put into stark relief decisions that are off-purpose and thus would make violating the purpose more difficult.

Real leaders calculate risk, but they choose their direction based on the current situation, facts, values, and wise counsel, *guided by the outcome they want*. They optimize information flow, decision making, and right action to achieve that outcome. They help members of their team set clear objectives with clear time frames, aligned with the overall purpose of the organization. They have the courage to make the right decisions based on their values and purpose.

My company has found over years of consulting that part of "building the bridge" of organizational transformation as you proceed is rapidly building behavioral alignment based on organizational and personal integrity that usually begins with the top leaders and spreads down through real leaders throughout the organization. A company in alignment can adapt to changing conditions and at the same time stabilize as it proceeds. This kind of self-initiated behavior of real leaders, aligned with the desired outcome, is the essence of being on-purpose.

Purpose-Based Language

Being on-purpose is moving the flashlight to a new spot. When it is illuminated, people can see the writing on the wall, the goals and the mission, and are better able to move through the uncertainty that surrounds us when we aim toward a better future. They can better see where they and others are on-purpose and off-purpose with the new direction. Thereby on-purpose behavior becomes much more likely, and so does closing the gaps.

This is why purpose is at the top of the Grinnell Organizational Vitality Model (figure 2 in chapter 1). Like a beacon at the top of a lighthouse, it is the guiding light that people can home in on as they prepare to jump out of the quit zone. Once your organization's purpose—and yours—is clear, then you can expand awareness and seek alignment. Without clear purpose, awareness is only haphazard and not very useful. With clear purpose, leaders and teams can sort the options that expanded awareness produces. Without clear purpose and without expanding awareness beyond current mind-sets and beliefs, alignment too is haphazard. Seeking and then finding alignment allows people to share the load and work in collaborative competence. Once everyone understands purpose and is aligned toward it, they can begin to act accountably with each other and with purpose through vertical teamwork and horizontal collaboration.

Here are some points to keep in mind as you as a leader point your flashlight at the wall for your followers:

1. Overuse the terms "on-purpose" and "off-purpose" to embed the concept. Tied with honest and respectful tone this will reduce off-purpose embarrassment, fear, and guilt. It will reduce dependence upon you for making all of the decisions or reinforcing other people's insecurity—all of which erode your ability to have the time you need as a leader.

2. Make clear to the people the logical connection between the values, beliefs, behavior, structures, and processes you are asking them to change and the approaching future. They must see that connection if they are to grasp the purpose, embrace the transformation, and jump into the unknown future. Make sure they understand the mid- and long-term benefit to them for making the choice to lead with you toward the envisioned future. Talk about the challenges and how you plan to address them.

3. Translate vision into a meaningful mission and core values, which together are your organization's purpose. The vision and purpose enable you to identify gaps; turn those gaps into objectives for change. Give them the best tactical picture you can. Objectives are what success looks like in the future as you change systems, processes, and culture. As-

sign each of the few critical objectives to an executive and have that executive pick a team capable of real leadership.

4. Paradoxically, in many cases, and if you have the luxury of some time, don't achieve the objectives too quickly. They are the anvil against which you can forge real leaders down in the organization. Staff them thoughtfully and arrange the process to challenge leaders so they can grow into real leadership, which is something savvy leaders are always cultivating for future demand. In other words you don't want to waste a crisis, contrived or surprising.

5. Use tools to help you focus. A few years ago my firm developed a process we call "Competitive Path Mapping™." It's a one-page flow diagram connecting the vision and mission to yearly goals and tactical objectives. This diagram shows how work being done on the organization addresses the future, how assignments connect with the purpose. It is a way to ensure that people know they are not just "breaking rocks" when you ask them to change the way they do things—they are "building a cathedral." It forces an organization to focus on a few key things.

6. Use your map to document current agreed-on targets. It should be a living document—as you learn and change, it changes so everyone knows how to be on-purpose throughout the process.

7. Hold regular accountability group reporting sessions on objectives. This is not a report card or a grading system, but rather a way for real leaders to tell the truth about progress and problems, and to ask for help early. Highlight and reward on-purpose results and respectfully and in a nonemotional way point out off-purpose behavior. It uses peer pressure and is a form of accountability to others and the organization that you don't get with one-on-one interactions.

Leadership Beyond Belief
Values-Based Leadership

Back in the late 1970s I had the great fortune to work at the National Humanistic Education Center in upstate New York in the beautiful Adirondacks. My job was to split wood getting ready for the 1980 Winter Olympics in Lake Placid. I would work late in the afternoons and early morning so I could attend some amazing programs given by some of the top "values educators" in the world: Sid Simon, Howard Kirshenbaum, and the Johnson brothers from the University of Minnesota, among many others. At that time there was a movement in the country to what was called "values clarification" and also resistance to it. Looking back, I didn't realize at the time how fundamental values are to the self-aware human being. In fact, that was at a time when I was twenty-five years old and wasn't very aware, just extremely curious. I wish I had paid more attention.

No discussion of purpose is complete without a consideration of values and their importance to leadership, organizational life, and, indeed, individuals' lives. Purpose is your new fully chosen three-foot circle on the wall. Values are the light beam guiding you through the uncertainty and darkened unknown of change—getting you from here to your chosen there.

Once we become aware that beliefs drive our perceptions, choices, and behaviors and that they are in large part learned through the process of socialization and experience, and further, once we know that the way we see and respond is based on our unconscious memory—and nothing else—we are at an interesting point in our lives. Some people call it an existential crisis, others like me call it an "existential breakthrough." That is, we are confronted with the task of choosing the rest of our lives. We can choose to change to address the future in a manner that will result in our getting the experience we want (although there are no guarantees), or we can go back to sleep and accept what we are programmed to experience. Either way is okay, but the existential question of "Who am I, and what do I want to do and experience in my life?" is the age-old question experienced by the lucky few (although it doesn't feel lucky at first). Not just individuals but also organizations ask these existential questions. As John Allison, former CEO of BB&T Bank, so succinctly said ("John

Being On-Purpose

Allison" 2011) in a statement that Mark Fernandes of Luck Companies later tweeted:

> [Leaders] create a sense of purpose . . . , and they live a set of principles [values] that enable that purpose to [become] reality.

As I said earlier, once we know that our perceptions and reactions are made up according to our beliefs, and that automated beliefs that were learned in the past drag us through the future, we can then make a choice—we can then become truly responsible for our lives and the organizations we lead. It takes a commitment to self-awareness, then creating a sense of purpose or meaning. The hard part is being ruthlessly honest with ourselves to see where we are out of alignment with our purpose, where our past beliefs do not serve our or our organization's purpose. This is where, according to Allison ("John Allison" 2011), a lot of organizations and the leaders who run them fail. They are unwilling to take an honest look at the reality they are living and leading.

I recently visited Luck Companies. John Stump, a good friend, long-term client, and CEO of Monitech, had told me he had met a fellow named Mark Fernandes (@markSFernandes) and said: "John, you have to meet this guy. You and he are amazingly aligned." Well, the stars (and our calendars) did align and I met him at the company's world headquarters near Richmond, Virginia, less than a week later. I had no idea of what I would find. His leadership development partner, Danielle, and Mark met with me for over two hours and we couldn't stop talking. He told me about an amazing personal life-and-death crisis that the third-generation owner of Luck Companies, Charlie Luck, had gone through that changed the course of their organization's history. Upon returning to work after a long sabbatical, Luck decided to continue to build the business on a set of core values established six years earlier. But to up the ante, the company would work diligently on developing a model for values-based leadership, invest heavily in embedding the model inside the company, and when the time was right, share the new body of work with the world. Mark told me it was an all-out bet: the leaders bet the house on a simple but profound value for people; that is, "doing good, making a difference in the lives of our associates, is the best path to doing well, personal and business performance. Simply put (and in the words of Charles Luck Jr., Charlie's grandfather, who founded the company): 'if you do right by your people, they will do right by you.'"

This decision recognized that the first principle that makes a values-driven organization work is self-awareness. On the cover of their employee handbook (which is like no other handbook I've ever seen) is a statement of another simple but profound value:

Leadership is a choice, not a title—a conscious *choice to work first on yourself to in turn positively impact the lives of those around you.*

Luck Companies' tagline or "brand statement," "Igniting Human Potential," is equally powerful for those who can truly see how human potential is released through self-awareness and behavior aligned with core values and purpose. Luck's tagline is the slam dunk of leadership, in my opinion. All organizations are based on the human beings who work in and lead them. To release human potential is to raise the power of the organization. And as previously pointed out, human potential is bound in false and most often unconscious beliefs about oneself that serve as limiters of our potential. Luck Companies' central value puts them truly at the leverage point. And their bottom lines seem to show it. Luck Companies are creating a center for leadership based on a profound vision: "To ignite human potential through values based leadership and to positively impact lives around the world."

Values are the basis of the path we choose through life. We may have myriad unconscious and conscious beliefs, but values are deeply felt commitments to taking the path that leads to what we want to paint on the canvas of our life. Beliefs drive organizations until leadership decides to choose values that fully align with purpose. Until then, outcome is happenstance and victim to the past. In this regard, changing organizational direction is not dissimilar to therapy. The best psychologists and psychiatrists know that all they do is work on the past in memory to help their clients create a better future.

Being On-Purpose

That is it: to examine what runs us on automatic and then take a stand to choose what we believe and value in spite of sometimes great resistance. It is the grand bet with one's life and leadership. Without chosen values, human organizations and the leaders who run them are adrift in a sea of uncertainty and constant change, clinging to the empty hope of their driftwood of beliefs. Mark Fernandes makes this point succinctly:

> Companies all around the world are being challenged to think about why they exist, the meaning they want to make, their mission or purpose. And in the process articulate a clear set of values that when adhered to, ensure the organization is living its mission while also delivering on its business unit visions, strategies and performance objectives.

A great number of companies espouse their values, but operate in a state of hypocrisy when pressure hits. The great ones don't. As leaders consciously commit to a set of values, and work to align those who follow them through hiring, on-boarding, communicating, training, and holding accountable, they need fewer policies. This is because when the organization's leadership is aligned around the same values, those leaders and their followers can "self-reference" the values, and make decisions and take actions in alignment with the strategy and objectives. This creates great agility and the possibly of innovative solutions that don't require executive management to do all the thinking. This is a great competitive advantage, when what the company deeply is and consciously values, that is, *believes*, is obvious to the customer.

There are many potential values one can choose. What are the ones you want to live and experience in your lifetime? What is the collective outcome you and your organization want to experience? What unconscious or unstated values are operating beneath the surface of awareness? Which continue to be in alignment and which are no longer viable in light of your direction and purpose? Who has the stomach to truly live them and who doesn't? Selecting values takes time, and aligning with them takes even more time and is hard work, as some people will not get the promotions they think they deserve as fast as they want them. Others who have been unseen will move up. Invisible sociopolitical contracts between boss and subordinates are violated and new ones formed. People can feel hurt. But the truth is, values misalignment is not good for the company or for the person who is operating in hypocrisy and out of alignment. The good news is that with self-awareness and the realization that humans can, in large part, create the outcomes they desire in their lives, they less rigidly hold onto beliefs formed earlier and choose values aligned with the future they choose.

Human potential is bound by false beliefs—most often by beliefs formed very early in our lives that limit how we see ourselves. Certainly they may not be fully aligned with what we want to experience. The beauty of values is that they are also beliefs, but unlike unconscious beliefs they are prioritized above other beliefs, "valued" more, and aligned with the experience we want to get in our lives. Organizations are the same as individuals; they hold myriad beliefs, often created early in the history of the company and reflecting a founder's perspective. Unlike Luck Companies, usually organizations form the unconscious values haphazardly and without consideration of purpose as people bring their own past random experiences to the organization. With a solid set of core values, consciously chosen and aligned with purpose and held in place by accountable leadership, the likelihood of an organization's success increases dramatically.

Our website at Grinnell Leadership has a simple phrase: "A changed mind is the bridge to transformation," and the first step in transformation is a change of mind. This is so true both personally and organizationally. Real transformation requires a reframing of who we are, our role, and our purpose, and most importantly it requires defining and living our values differently, with less hypocrisy. This is a significant undertaking. Some transformations are forced on an organization, as can be the case with mergers or acquisitions. It always amazes me how the financially savvy can make great strategic decisions to improve position and capture a market, and ignore the significant realignment of values and relationships with purpose that is necessary in order to avoid losing the human value. Headhunters hover over these situations looking for high performers who "feel" out of alignment and are ready to exit, often to a worse situation, only because of the discomfort and uncertainty they experience due to a perceived or real misalignment of values. Unfortunately, many leave because management hasn't taken the time to understand the organization's values and therefore can't articulate them or demonstrate them with integrity.

When a leader sets an intention to transform an organization and his or her approach to leadership, that leader will often create a clear picture of the future state in practical business terms. Such leaders will identify what they do, to whom they will sell it, and how much they will charge. They may even discuss how they will differentiate themselves from the competition and discuss what percentage of organic versus acquisition growth they will use to reach the new performance level. I have found, though, that it is the rare company that will define the *values* that its leaders believe will create sustainable value.

John Allison, when he was CEO at BB&T, beginning in the late 1980s and through the '90s implemented a fast-growth phase of the company. As banking went national across state borders for the first time, it became a "grow or be acquired" situation. He set up a brilliant growth strategy, but, maybe more importantly, he and his organization created a set of values that were the building blocks of success. These were values they lived by. They held true to their values; clearly they promoted their use, and often used those values to make both important and everyday decisions. Their commitment worked and BB&T is one of the most successful banks in the country.

In fact, when asked in an interview what he considered his greatest success, Allison responded, "My biggest business success was developing an organization that ran on fundamental, ethical principles." Those fundamental principles lay the foundation for a successful company, as well as for successful persons, he asserted, and lacking them will ultimately cause failure. With those fundamental principles in place, he reiterated, one will succeed.

A recent book by a noted executive and a marketing professor effectively makes these points about values and purpose, and how important they are to a successful company. In *Conscious Capitalism*, the cofounder and co-CEO of Whole Foods Market, John Mackey, and Raj Sisodia make a case for businesses motivated by serving people through their products, and not just by profits. "Purposeful companies," they assert, "ask questions such as these: Why does our business exist? Why does it need to exist? What core values animate the enterprise and unite all of our stakeholders? Higher purpose and shared core values unify the enterprise and elevate it to higher degrees of motivation, performance, and ethical commitment" (2013:34).

Values need to be part of the most significant leadership decisions and actions. In fact, not only are "purpose and mission" a basis of decision making but alignment with our values is as well. For example, one of the most significant actions executives make is their yearly planning meeting. Sometimes this takes the form of a true "strategic planning" session where the organization takes an outside-in look from the customers and market back to operations. This is usually a process to begin finding market adjustments. Sometimes misalignment can be found between the organization's intentions and values and the customer experience. However, on a more routine basis, "business planning" is really an inside-out look at operations, how people are working, and where the organization stands relative to its goals and objectives. This is a perfect time to look at the alignment of core values with employee behavior and worldview. For this we often recommend a leadership climate study we call a VitalOrgScan™. Within this organizational inquiry process, we help executive management spot misalignment not only with the business plans but also with core values and leadership behavior.

Setting Core Values

Core values must be set at three levels. The first is conceptual alignment, which means it makes good business sense in terms of where we are going, as well as the experience we want to get in our lifetime. At this level values can be espoused, but not lived. It is a starting point for most discussions about values.

The second level is ensuring there is behavioral alignment. Operating at this level will get you into the game and, as Jim Collins in his book *Good to Great* says, "a seat on the bus." That is, people behave in a manner that demonstrates the core values of our organization. Behavioral alignment is good, but we can, in fact, espouse

34

values, but behave as "actors." At this level, the values are not what we call "lived" beliefs. There is some value in the concept of "fake it until you make it." At first, when changing behavior, we can feel like actors, but eventually the innate value must be genuinely "felt" for there to be a lasting commitment. If this doesn't happen, it indicates that there may be a fundamental misalignment between a leader, his or her character, and the company he or she works for.

The third level is "heartfelt." It is part innate, as deeply held beliefs guide a sense of knowing that the values are right for you. When there is heartfelt alignment, it is a commitment of one's life, energies, and focus. This gives a tremendous advantage to the organization as it goes through transformation. You may not know exactly how you will get there, the plans and procedures are changing, and you are "building the bridge as you walk on it." But the core values are your "guides in the night." They are your chosen channel markers that allow you to feel a sense of certainty about your experience, the path you are following, and the outcome you want for your life. The leap of faith and "living the values" is heartfelt. What this means is that there is no other way you would want to live and spend your time at work. When you align your values with what you do, it will often affect the way you live outside work.

As a young consultant, I was assigned the account training frontline supervisors at a major corporation. Its core value was and still is safety. They were and still are the benchmark for safety. People around town could all tell its employees as they would wear their goggles and hard-toed shoes when mowing their grass at home. The first day I consulted I was warned to hold the handrail and in unison the group I was working with told me not to lean back in my chair. They acted with integrity and had absolutely no qualms about saying and doing the right thing according to their core value.

As another example, I once worked on retainer for Charlie Davidson, CEO of JA Jones Construction in Charlotte, North Carolina. The gift Charlie gave me was his unwavering commitment to and deep understanding of integrity. I haven't been the same since I worked for him. He helped me raise my bar on "doing the right thing even when no one is looking or would ever find out."

The Erosion of Values

There is a great little book written by Elliot Aronson and one of his graduate students (Tavris and Aronson 2007). I have always loved the title: *Mistakes Were Made (but Not by Me)*. In this wonderfully written and readable, research-based book, they point out that the violation of integrity with our core values seldom happens in one big change in behavior, but rather by "small cuts of the knife" over time. This makes me think of the Enron debacle that resulted in the unintended consequences of not only the waste of time and money, and increased taxation spent in producing the Sarbanes-Oxley law, but the even more devastating result of thousands of people losing not only their jobs but also their life savings. I doubt if Ken Lay and his gang conspired to hurt those people. In fact, I am willing to bet Ken probably went to the religious institution of his faith, donated to charities, and so on. He very likely saw himself as a virtuous man, but over the years he had gradually and repeatedly violated integrity (alignment) with his values or had not required accountability, thereby "suboptimizing" a value for making money that turned into greedy culture (yet they had all their "official" values written and publicized widely). Aronson points out that once human beings get so far outside their idealized views of themselves (identity), they tend to go blind, rationalize, and magically see themselves wrongly—as still that idealized identity. At that point all hell breaks loose.

Some will disagree with me here, but my view based on my observations and reading (and not personal experience) is that Bernie Madoff and his billion-dollar fiasco likely reenacted the same scenario—a good person gone wrong, and in this case creating very bad outcomes for many. Values are critically important, but so is the stomach to *not* violate them—even in small ways. The story about how slowly turning up the heat of the water to a boil will cook the frog and the frog will not realize it may not be true, but the concept is when it comes to human nature and values erosion.

Leading Values

The price of integrity is constant vigilance.
—Oliver Wendell Holmes

Organizations are no different. If executive management espouses only the values and doesn't live them and have the courage to uphold them, then the organization's potential is compromised. I heard that Jack Welch was asked at his departure from GE, "If you could have done one thing differently, what would it have been?" He answered, "I would have gotten rid of the high-performing moneymakers faster when they weren't aligned with our core values." He saw the long-term consequence of retaining people who are misaligned with the organization's values. It takes courage to lead; without the courage to hold people accountable, particularly executive management and high performers, you are likely enjoying short-term success, or less success than you could be.

Things you can do to strengthen your core values:

1. Make sure you know what your core values are and use them repeatedly to make tough decisions. Talk openly about your decisions and how the values influenced what you did. Managers often resort to the hard facts and numbers and ignore this. Don't.
2. Communicate the core values over and over and over again. Bring them up in meetings, test decisions with them. Put them in your administrative processes as well as in your marketing materials.
3. Hold people accountable to them. When a violation occurs, collect your facts, deal with it directly, and don't waste time.
4. When someone admits hypocrisy, if the violation is not too egregious and you think the cause was lack of awareness, forgive and move forward.
5. Off-load anyone who has such misaligned behavior that key personnel or clients might see your company in a different light than you want.
6. Make the values discussion a part of every planning process, strategic or otherwise.
7. If you want to alter the culture and values, focus on the positive. It's much faster and better to set expectations,

what the behaviors associated with the new values look like, than to spend time trying to "fix" the old.

8. Be proud of your values. Demonstrate the cause and effect of your values. When success occurs look at how the values played a part in it. Publicize it widely.

9. All technical training and financial and administrative decisions should be aligned with the values to highlight purpose and enterprise thinking.

10. Incorporate deep-belief-level leadership development into your core curriculum. With this, people will know they have a choice and will not blindly believe the values. The choice for one's life is what counts, not what the crowd wants to do. Individual commitment is what you want.

Leading with a Purpose

Leading transformation is difficult and can be scary—it means being one of the first to consciously dive headlong into an unknown future, feeling vulnerable and stretching with newly chosen, untested beliefs and behavior. But it's also one of the most exhilarating actions you can take—embracing the specific uncertainty of doing what hasn't been done before—in hope of creating a better future for yourself, your organization, and society. Purpose and your values light up the dark path before you toward that brighter future that lies ahead.

When you join purpose to values, you are well on your way to succeeding in your personal life—to having the life you want. Your organization is also on the path to success, and to making a positive impact in our fast-changing, challenging world. And you are transforming not only your organization but yourself, into a real leader.

Structuring Purpose

Here are some recommendations for instilling a sense of purpose and direction:

Being On-Purpose

1. Using the template shared in chapter 8, develop a draft purpose or mission statement with the group responsible for its achievement. Once this is done, create behavioral team working agreements that support success in reaching the purpose.

2. Read Patrick Lencioni's *Five Dysfunctions of a Team* (2002) and his newest book, *The Advantage* (2012), and talk about the chapter "Create Clarity" in the latter.

3. Make handouts of the Grinnell Organizational Vitality Model and hold discussion about on- and off-purpose behavior. Be prepared to tie off-purpose behavior to organizational loss and waste, and to entropy. Ask for some examples of past off-purpose behavior. What kinds of behavior does our culture support that are off-purpose?

4. Periodically do an anonymous survey of the team's behavioral working agreements and values. Don't focus it on the individual; focus the questions on the team. Have the team discuss how to improve going forward.

5. Use the terms "on-purpose" and "off-purpose" in your everyday decisions, actions, and feedback sessions. Couch your performance system's periodic feedback in terms of being off-purpose and on-purpose, not good or bad, right or wrong.

Chapter 3
Acting Accountably
Courage or Compromise of Leadership

Open dialogue has produced a purpose and path forward toward your company's one- and three-year goals. In addition, you had a great session building a tactical plan with metrics and milestones for reaching your goals. You and all members of the executive team as well as followers below seem aligned around that plan and path. Many executives believe their job is done and they can dispense assignments and wait for the results. Wrong. The job has just started—and the most difficult challenge lies ahead—changing minds. Unless new beliefs and new habits are accepted and demonstrated then your effort to change course is likely to flounder and ultimately fail. Time and again in my experience, companies and individuals who clearly saw what direction they needed to take to succeed and who rallied followers around a common purpose neglected to follow through in implementing the new plan by holding themselves accountable. In turn, they needed to work with others as leaders getting others to "hold themselves accountable."

Everyone is the key word here: it means subordinates and peers but it also means *you*. Just as awareness begins with self-awareness and builds from there to awareness of others' motivations, for leaders, accountability starts with themselves and then spreads out and down through the organization—the choice to be accountable.

Acting Accountably

> *Are you one of those that will get up at 2 a.m.*
> *to close the barn door when no one else will or*
> *can?*

Five years after a new CEO took over a struggling company, he had turned it around through his will and talent. It had now become a model for other companies in the conglomerate his company was part of. Though successful, he was miserable. He wanted to spend more time with his kids. He had promised himself and others that he would finally make changes in his organization, delegating more responsibility and authority to subordinates, in order to free more time for him to spend with his family. Now his wife pointed out that he had made this promise to her a year earlier, but nothing had changed.

The CEO realized that he had not held himself accountable to his intention. He also saw that if he continued acting the same way, he would create increasingly negative consequences not only for himself and his family but also for the company as he became more of a bottleneck. The executives on his leadership team had greatly improved, or so he thought, but he saw now that they, too, had become a decision bottleneck as they hadn't built accountability into the organization below them, a key challenge to building a vital organization. As a result, they—and he—were overwhelmed with responsibility. Someone had to carry the load, and when those below did not, it fell to the executives. As the executive team continued to "overmanage," their subordinates did the same. People were crying to be "empowered" yet the status quo remained. They too didn't know how to empower themselves by freeing up their time through effective delegation and gain a time payment. They didn't know it wasn't possible to be empowered . . . but rather they had to free up their time by being leaders of the enterprise instead of overmanaging. This would create a vacuum of sorts until subordinates who had delegated into a time payment could assume that which the executives currently managed.

Examining his own behavior, the CEO became aware that he tended to give people who weren't performing as they should a long time to improve, endlessly coaching them rather than replacing them. Just like his executive team who emulated him, he didn't challenge with progressive responsibility. And when he did he didn't hold himself accountable to give them timely positive and critical feedback. The unintended consequence of this behavior was that he was tired and miserable. If he persisted in this behavior, he realized, the company was not going to be on firm footing for the future.

Failure to hold oneself accountable to the organization's purpose usually produces unintended consequences—and most often they are not good ones. Without accountability, habitual behavior kicks back in, regardless of the clarity of vision and the incisiveness of the plan. In spite of the best of intentions, followers and the leaders themselves will regress to the mean; they'll go back to business as usual.

Normal Crazy Leadership

Years ago while working at Farr Associates, Inc., we would, with "tongue in cheek," use a term that I have modified over the years and have come to greatly appreciate. We now use it to describe a type of leadership that occurs in most organizations. We call it "normal crazy leadership." This doesn't mean "crazy crazy" or "really crazy," just ordinary, common, normal run-of-the-mill human leadership crazy. Normal crazy leadership has three components, and the first echoes habitual behavior, which I discuss in chapter 7: creating negative unintended consequences and dissatisfying experiences for yourself and others you associate with over and over. The other two components are that you actually want what you create and that you don't know you are doing it.

These other factors are counterintuitive. Why would we want to create negative unintended consequences of leadership and dissatisfying experiences? And if we want them, how can we not know it? To answer these questions, which I discuss in more detail in chapter 7, consider these points: people tend to act on beliefs formed early in life, actions that conform to the direction of their ego's defense mechanisms, and the motivations for these actions tend to remain hidden to them until they work toward self-awareness. You unconsciously want the result your behavior is producing and you are unwilling—or unable—to act to correct a belief and the associated habitual action that do not serve your new purpose. The behavior and outcome is familiar and habitual. In other words, you can be acting out of our own perception of "good and right" behavior, but in reality are just following the dictates of your unaware beliefs down the path of familiar experience, which is often not the path we want to be on. This is why feedback and transparency as illustrated in chapter 7 by the Johari Window is so very important to personal leadership and organizational vitality.

The CEO in the example I just related had a clear vision of what would bring his company success and his family happiness, but he was unable or unwilling to take action. Thus, in both his personal and professional life, he continued to experience negative and dissatisfying outcomes: normal but crazy leadership behavior. When that behavior manifests among leaders as normal crazy leadership, the likelihood that the leader him- or herself as well as followers will exercise accountability on their own becomes small. Leaders well know that "the buck stops here"; the flip side is that accountability starts here.

Accountability Begins and Ends with Self

We often hear the word *accountability* used in organizations, but it is largely not understood—very likely because people don't really want to understand it. We hear terms like "I hold my people accountable" or a frustrated executive will scream, "hold them accountable." In reality, the only person one can hold accountable is oneself. This is *not* a play on words. Human beings are volitional and make both conscious and unconscious choices based upon habits. All a leader can do is hold himself accountable to his role. A leader can ask a follower to do a certain function. He or she can also provide timely feedback and eventually, if performance is bad enough, can let the person go. An example may sound like this:

> *Manager (to follower): Please hold yourself accountable to achieve this goal for our organization. I will set up a reporting process that I would like you to work with. I will also hold myself accountable to perform my role and give you feedback on a timely and accurate basis as it relates to your performance. And if you decide to not align and work in a manner that leads to your and the organization's success after repeated coaching, I will hold myself accountable to let you go.*

In reality, *that's all a leader can do.* The follower can choose to not do what is requested or do it well. The power to achieve the goal resides in the follower not the leader. This accurate process that puts the power where it belongs is often violated as managers assume themselves the motive force and the most accountable. Procrastination and "leadership lag" in giving timely, respectful critical feedback is the other major violation—the leader doesn't remain accountable to his or her goal.

Accountability, in addition to not being fully understood, has other baggage. After all, hearing that you're accountable for something puts pressure on you; the implication is that there are consequences, and in the control-authority model most organizations in our culture operate within, the subtle emphasis is mostly negative. True, accountability is a way of sharing and feeling the consequences of failure—but it's also a way of sharing the consequences and feeling of success. We feel the uncertainty and risk associated with accountable leadership and followership, but we also get the satisfaction of achievement. Without accountability, an endeavor or an organization will operate with less vitality and is much less likely to succeed, as people don't really understand their true role and value to the organization. With it, the likelihood of success goes way up.

Acting Accountably

Many of us have used the word *accountability* for years and understood that it expressed an important concept, but haven't really thought that concept through fully.

I recently reached out to some people who know quite a bit about the subject: owners of small businesses, CEOs of successful larger companies, and other senior executives, as well as a professor of leadership and business administration at a major university. I asked them what accountability means to them, and as expected, received some insightful and useful answers. Almost all said that accountability is a way to know that an individual or organization is making progress toward an objective. The more objective and measurable the gauging of that progress is, the more accountable it is—and we are.

"Accountability is the feedback mechanism that links outcomes to the expectations of responsibility," said Walt Yourstone, former U.S. Navy submarine captain and commander of the Kings Bay Nuclear Submarine Base in St. Mary's, Georgia. Now president of VT Milcom, he says feedback is an important part of accountability. We'll come back to it, but for now, consider that though accountability often seems a cold, calculated, metric-based process, it is actually an effective way for human beings to "feel" not only the consequences of failure but the glory and reward of winning, the feeling that entrepreneurs and small business owners especially experience. They know all too well that if they don't succeed, they may have to sell the house they love and their kids may not be able to go to college. Accountability is the way we can get people who work in larger organizations to feel what those entrepreneurs and small business owners feel every day they go to work. It is a movement away from feelings of entitlement and complacency.

Accountability enables us to cement the products of awareness and alignment to our purpose. "If done correctly," Yourstone observed, "accountability is the process leaders can use to provide experiences that modify beliefs, thereby driving new behaviors, or reward and recognize desired behaviors—ingraining those behaviors to establish an organization's culture."

Accountability is not easy. "Accountability is essential to organizational health, but it requires planning, discipline, and time," said

45

John Stump, CEO of Monitech. "Making the time to establish norms for the group as well as goals and metrics at the organization, business unit, and individual level and the requisite daily, weekly, monthly, quarterly follow-through with the entire organization is a lot of work."

Responsibility and Accountability

Accountability is inseparably tied to responsibility. Responsibility has a couple of senses, and both apply to accountability: we are responsible *for* something, and we are responsible *to* someone or something. We're all familiar with being responsible for achieving a goal. Kevin Sowers, former CEO of Duke University Medical Center and current CEO of Johns Hopkins Health System, phrased this succinctly: "Your job has a specific set of responsibilities and tasks for which you are accountable to your boss." This responsibility can be quite broad and significant. "As a senior executive you have the ultimate accountability for the overall performance of the organization," Sowers noted.

Yet accountability goes beyond this basic sense of responsibility. Defining it as the duty to accomplish a task can leave out something important. "Accountability must at its heart acknowledge personal ownership of an act—intended or unintended," said a senior director of military programs in one of the largest defense contractors. "A position may make a person responsible for an outcome but may not specifically attach personal and more intimate ownership."

Completing an assignment successfully may be an achievement, but accountability in this sense means leaders bring more to that assignment than just the ability to execute it. "Responsibility implies 'my name is attached to that' or 'I'm in the chain of command on that' rather than I personally have committed to a promised result or action on *x* by a certain time," said Bruce Clarke, CEO of Capital Associated Industries. "'The buck stops here' because I'm the manager versus a personal commitment to the project or topic from design through execution." Though responsibility and accountability are quite similar, said Lee Grubb, associate professor of management and director of the Leadership and Professional Development Program for the College of Business at East Carolina University, there is one tremendous difference: "Accountability includes the notion of honor." Someone can be responsible for a task and then not fully accept his or her role in an unfavorable outcome, he pointed out. Holding oneself accountable means accepting responsibility for the outcome.

Perhaps the distinction boils down to position versus attitude. "Responsibility is defined by your job or role in life," Sowers said. "How you respond to it determines your understanding of accountability."

We're also all familiar with being responsible to someone or something—our boss, a board of directors, the organization itself. Here too, accountability goes beyond this basic sense. In being responsible to someone or something beyond ourselves, we glimpse the ultimate purposes of our work and our lives. "At the foundation of accountability is serving," said Al Petrangeli, president of Georgia Division of Balfour Beatty Construction—"yourself, others, God, etc. It's contributing. It's being proactive. It's a commitment. It's going forward."

Ensuring Accountability

By and large, the leaders I surveyed pointed to self-awareness as the foundation for demanding accountability from oneself. Ensuring accountability requires "true self-awareness based on continuous, cold, dispassionate self-assessment," said one, "facing me as I am, not what I wish I were or what others think I am." It requires "having a clear understanding of your responsibilities and an accurate knowledge of the results you are achieving," said Yourstone, "and the discipline to assess the two in the proper context, without prejudice. This is not easy—it requires looking at our own performance honestly, without distortion."

When a leader does make that accurate self-assessment, he or she still needs to act on it to be fully accountable. "I make sure that the behavioral norms apply equally to everyone in the organization, including myself," Stump said. "As an example, I was two minutes late to a staff meeting yesterday and a colleague publicly called me out on it as I had requested earlier. Another asked me why [I was late], and I replied, 'no excuse.' The group laughed, because early on when we were establishing our leadership team I had called out others who were late and told them that excuses like 'traffic' were not ok."

Leaders need insight as well into "how their value system is driving their behaviors and actions," Sowers said. "Assure you understand what values are the key drivers for you personally. Understand when those personal values and leadership traits become your greatest weakness." Ideally, the leader's personal values align with those of the organization, "but in some instances, leaders' values drive different behaviors and actions which are in direct conflict with the organizational values." This may be one of the most important aspects of accountability, and that is highlighting misalignment. Here's an example from my experience.

Years ago I worked with an executive who was brilliant and talented, and had an exceptionally well thought out vision for the future of their organization. He asked us to help him develop an execution plan to deliver the vision and values he espoused. I quickly saw that he was great at planning, but when it came down to giving timely and useful feedback in a direct, respectful way, he was completely unable to do so. He didn't hold himself accountable with this critical element of leadership. I did all I could with technique and approaches I had developed over the previous twenty years of consulting and coaching, but I couldn't get him to give feedback or replace the executives who were not getting the job done. Eventually the inevitable happened: the CEO stepped in and very sadly let him go. He got another job, but was shortly let go there too. He had an unconscious value or belief that was well rationalized that would not allow him to be truly accountable to his role and do the right thing, and he ended up always holding the bag. He valued people, and he valued peace and harmony, so much so that he could not make tough decisions; this had a negative impact on both him and on the organization. Not understanding that accountability starts and ends

Acting Accountably

with oneself and that personal beliefs of which we are unaware and personal unexamined values will misalign us and
thereby sabotage us if we don't have awareness creates such
an outcome. You have to know the old box to get out of it.

Accountability has two drivers, Clarke said: the internal desire
to achieve and the external pressure not to fail. To ensure accountability in himself, he said, "I only take on important projects that I
believe in and really want to achieve (the first driver) and that I
commit to in front of others (the external pressure). When one of
those is missing, my chance of failure goes way up."

For Grubb, honor is the key. Leaders "must be willing to be honest not only with themselves but with all other parties. I attach honor
to many things, such as my family, organization, coworkers, the
academic environment, and not least of all, myself. If I am not willing
to be held accountable, and am also not willing to hold others accountable, I am belittling the honor and trust others have for me that
I have worked so hard to achieve."

He related a personal example of insisting on accountability that
required patience and persistence:

One of my roles in private industry was managing a large
customer service department for a third party administrator
of health care benefits. It was a difficult time for the industry
and the organization and the company had recently gone
through an unpleasant round of layoffs.

The supervisors who reported to me came to me and explained that our employees had very low morale and were
concerned about the potential for more layoffs. Production
was falling and I needed to do something to ensure that the
employees had some level of reassurance and could again
begin concentrating on their work or things would get worse. I
met with my boss, who assured me that the employees were
safe and that there would be no more layoffs. I scheduled a
number of meetings on that Friday to relay the information to
the employees to decrease their concern and help them rally
with the positive news.

Leadership Beyond Belief

The meetings seemed to go well and everyone left that Friday afternoon with their heads held high and with a new sense of direction. That next Monday, my boss called me into her office and told me I had to lay off six of my employees. The news sickened me and my head was spinning. The appropriate decisions were made and the shocking news delivered to the employees and with great difficulty, I broke the news to the ill-fated six.

At that point I had behaved responsibly and I had conducted the business of the organization to the best of my ability. However, I felt accountable for the well-being of my employees, and everyone's world had been turned upside down. I could have continued to work there without changing my routine, but again, I felt accountable to my employees, the ones who stayed and the ones who were to be let go. I needed to do more.

I remained in my position long enough to ensure that each of the six employees being laid off was hired locally by other companies, and only at that time did I feel like I could say I had fulfilled the commitment I had to all of the employees who held me accountable for the success of the various team members. Having satisfied my team and myself, I tendered my resignation.

The Myth of Holding Others Accountable

Holding subordinates accountable seems straightforward: you give them a task and require them to complete it, and if they don't, they suffer the consequences. But it's not so simple. As pointed out earlier the only person who can hold one accountable is oneself. In the first place, you *want* consequences from actions for your organization—positive ones. Viewing accountability from this perspective instead of simply as a negative force brings into focus its value in the process of transforming an organization. "When accountability is seen as a positive tool that can foster development and full communication as opposed to the 'witch hunt' that it is sometimes perceived to be (or in fact might really be)," said one executive, "the organization's potential can be unleashed and success beyond our most optimistic hope can be realized." Great potential can be reached when the leader him- or herself becomes truly accountable and communicates through demonstrating such real accountability.

Many executives don't know how to go about unleashing this potential. How many times have you seen assignments that are too vague and outcomes that are not measurable, resulting in subjective judgments about performance? How often have you seen poor performance not handled or feedback not given in a timely manner, with executives either doing the work their subordinates should have done or becoming so frustrated that they erupt in angry tirades? Not letting employees know how their performance falls short gives them no way to improve it, and outbursts are unlikely to align followers with the organization's purpose in the long run. If these patterns continue, often the high-performing people will start looking for work elsewhere, as they are tired of carrying the weight for those who don't care or who feel entitled.

Accountability can be a powerful tool for transforming a negative situation into a positive one. Accountability must be maintained and monitored throughout. One executive provided an example from his own experience:

A key team player who was extremely talented and essential to the company was having trouble working with others on his team and peers in the company. When we sat down to talk about it, it became clear that this person was not comfortable working in a company that was undergoing the magnitude of change that our company was. This person also felt— correctly—that others on the team were not supporting him.

When we looked at the problem, there were many contributing factors, including his personal behaviors and often unreasonably high expectations of himself and others. He was put on notice that if he did not change, he would be let go. This was extremely difficult, as we had invested almost two years in getting him up to speed and he was making huge progress and had unlimited scientific potential. We are in a unique business with significant technical requirements. I was convinced he would not succeed and was greatly concerned that we would not be able to recover from his departure without suffering significant losses.

He is working better with his teammates, yet is now up and down, requiring regular feedback when he is on and off purpose. He seems to have made the commitment to change, but his behavior and emotions are lagging behind his intention. We have set clear expectations and dates for his performance, and are taking steps to minimize a downside if he doesn't make the behavioral shift. We will make the right decision for the organization.

Metrics of Success

For an organization to reach toward its potential, staying on-purpose in setting out and pursuing its goals is critical. For people to hold themselves accountable, "one must provide clear goals," Grubb said. "One may not always be able to provide clear instructions, but the goals should be articulated in such a way that success or failure will be easily recognized." The word itself holds the clue: "account-able."

Here we can see the importance of metrics in laying out those goals. "Goals that are truly *smart* goals (which is a mnemonic device that means 'specific, measurable, attainable, relevant, and time-bound,' established by George Duran in 1981) will have metrics associated with them, and progress toward accomplishing the goals can be measured," said Yourstone. "Consider the case of a proposal manager who isn't meeting his responsibility to prepare winning proposals. Feedback that can tie back to his actual proposal win rates is much more effective than just telling him he has to try harder." If the leader isn't prepared with metrics, he added, conversations between leaders and followers are based on "emotion and speculation."

To use metrics most effectively to gauge performance, the leader must let followers know from the beginning, and clearly, what standards he or she will use to assess them. This requires "clarity in

Acting Accountably

setting expectations verbally and in writing," said Sowers. "You have to take the time to communicate with them, in an open and honest manner, with the facts," said Yourstone. "You constantly have to seek out opportunities to create experiences for your team that will either reinforce or modify behavior by influencing their belief systems."

Equally important is keeping tabs on progress and keeping in touch throughout the process. This, again, can be a positive experience rather than the grown-up equivalent of going to the principal's office. "Create check-in on key milestones," Sowers advised, "to create an ongoing monitoring system that supports both you and the other person." This is often difficult for busy executives, or their personality is such that this type of important routine is challenging. If this is the case, this is so important that they should assign someone to help them with this step, but the actual feedback and "holding accountable" cannot be delegated.

Paradoxically, allowing room for failure is an important step in this process. The essence of accountability is trust, said Grubb. "One can behave responsibly and not have the trust of others, but to be truly accountable, one must be trusted." This trust needs to flow both ways. "People need to have a trusting relationship with others where there is no fear of failing based on honest effort. We need to have an open environment where we can learn from both the successes and failures of others with whom we work." Another executive echoed this viewpoint: "The fair application of accountability must embrace tolerance of mistakes and a commitment to work through them and learn and grow from this process." It is important to learn from the mistake, and this requires awareness, which is dependent on timely, useful, and accurate feedback, which leads to insight.

As a leader, you must figure out how to reinforce your followers' ability to receive—and provide—honest feedback so they can learn to handle emotional discomfort while building trust and more open communication. Understanding how to do this can be difficult, so using an experienced outside catalyst to facilitate this process can help. A first step could be the use of anonymous surveys administered after followers have developed enough awareness to hear ego-challenging data delivered by a third party. The two goals of this should be to educate followers (and yourself) on, first, how to recognize defensive behavior and, second, what to do to move forward to find honest alignment with purpose. Difficult-to-hear feedback can be the anvil against which you can build greater strength for dialogue on the team. When selecting an outside consultant or catalyst, keep in mind that the catalyst must not fear strong emotion or conflict, and must be able to use conflict soundly to bring about healthy growth in your team.

Response-able or Not

If a leader is going to hold him- or herself accountable so followers will know how to hold themselves accountable, then that leader needs to provide them with the resources they need to succeed. The obvious ones are tangible—money and people. But other, less visible tools are just as important. To be "account-able" requires that they also be "response-able." That is, they have to have the inner resources and capability to respond successfully. Often this is ignored by the overzealous manager focused on "checking the box" and quickly achieving his or her goals.

Responsibility of the leader is accompanied by authority, Yourstone pointed out, "authority to take actions, make decisions, and expend resources (funding, manpower, time)—authority to execute actions to fulfill the responsibility." The yoking of these concepts has implications when leaders are communicating expectations to followers. "A key point to make: if I am the leader of an organization responsible for some objectives, I can delegate authority down into the organization to enable decision making by the folks who carry out the daily actions, enabling their success (what I call getting power to the edge).

"I can also place responsibility on these decision makers (and should) in order to hold them accountable for both their successes and shortfalls." True, the buck stops with the leader, but knowing this can lead to missteps. Yourstone elaborated on this point:

What I cannot do is transfer the responsibility that my superiors placed on my shoulders. I am ultimately responsible for the outcomes of the organization and will be held accountable for them. This is one of the reasons why immature leaders resort to micromanagement. They understand that ultimate responsibility rests with them, so they are uneasy in giving up control and inject themselves into the decision-making process. They create a choke point in the organization—limiting the group to the pace of decision making by a single person.

To succeed, organizational leaders need to ensure several things:
- "They must create a decision-making environment that empowers the organization to make decisions, by creating a detailed understanding of the organization's vision, mission, goals, and value system," Yourstone said. "This will align the decision making throughout the organization to a direction that will achieve the organization's vision and the desired objectives." With clarity followers can make aligned decisions without as much oversight by management (time payment for management).
- They must make sure the ones to whom responsibility is delegated actually have the resources and time needed to hold them successfully accountable.
- "They must establish a system of monitoring and checks and balances that enables the leader to become part of the decision making for the critical decisions," Yourstone said.
- They must develop a reporting system that does not "micromanage" but allows the leader to know where the delegated duty is so that there are no surprises, good or bad. An executive client, Tim Gelbar, aptly calls this system a manager's touchpoints. Many people wrongly think that reporting is micromanagement when it isn't. This needs to be made explicit and the reporting process established by agreement of both sides.

Leaders who can empower followers through sharing the organization's vision can enable them to claim ownership of the organization's goals, which is an effective approach to both alignment and accountability. Clarke, for instance, said he ensures accountability in followers "by giving people fairly wide latitude in defining their objective (so they believe in it) and keeping their performance visible in our regular one-to-ones. I'd rather they accomplish several important things we both believe in than far fewer things that I primarily believe in."

Ambrose Dittloff, president of Carocon Corporation, emphasizes what he calls "quiet leadership": "The quiet leader may be the antithesis of the hard-charging, frontline, sword-out leader (who, in the older days was likely the first to go down!). In my mind, the quiet leader is more effective and will achieve a culture of empowerment."

He lists five tenets of quiet leadership:

1. Ensuring that motivated, capable people are in the right positions—strive to have all high performers.
2. Allowing people to do their best with the presumption that they want to do their best and achieve.
3. Empowering people with the freedom to make decisions that support their mission and objectives.
4. Supporting people with tools, training, skill development, and appropriate rewards.
5. Staying out of the way by quietly encouraging, critiquing, and providing rear-echelon support—removing obstacles that get in people's way.

Mutual Accountability

In chapter 1 I discussed the One-Team model. When an organization develops a One-Team, its members who work together smoothly develop a sense of accountability to do their role well so others can be successful too. When leaders and followers all understand intuitively how they are connected and depend on each other, they understand why accountability is crucial and what it entails. So if you can focus on building a team—an organization where people feel like teammates and feel responsible for their teammates' success—accountability will follow.

Acting Accountably

How do you build such a team in business? In addition to making it clear that accountability is a personal decision, the commonly understood elements of communication, honest feedback, transparency, and mutual support are essential; making highly visible the organization's purpose, vision, values, and goals is paramount. These characteristics must apply not only between people within a unit but horizontally (that is, across units and to customers) and vertically (that is, between leaders and followers). This task may seem daunting, but if you think about how championship-winning sports teams function, you realize that building a One-Team can be done, and you see the importance of everyone's understanding and sharing a common purpose and common goals. The idea of winning the World Series—or in business—is easily graspable, after all, and teammates quickly and intuitively understand what kind of performance and what mutual support are necessary.

The sports analogy transfers easily to business. If you played basketball, did you want to play with a star who always took difficult jump shots rather than pass to a teammate with a chance for a better shot? A responsible captain or coach would let the star know quickly that the team could not tolerate that behavior, and that is "holding oneself accountable." Choosing your team in business is similar. In listing three requirements for accountability, Grubb said that one is honor in followers as well as in self: "One must surround one's self with honorable people who are willing to be accountable for their actions and outcomes." In listing "encouragement, coaching, and leading by example" as ways to ensure accountability, Petrangeli added, "place myself with others who share my values and thus my value in accountability, and separate from those who have trouble with accountability."

When I attended East Carolina University, I played football under Coach Pat Dye. During the 1975 season, we lost our first three games. We were expected to contend for a conference championship, so these losses puzzled Coach Dye. In frustration, he said to one of my teammates, "I just can't figure it out. How could we lose those games with the talent we have this year?" My teammate didn't have an answer, but he pledged to the coach that he and his friends on the team would do whatever was necessary to turn the team around.

That response, Dye told me later, made him realize what the problem was. We weren't a unified team; we were a collection of four or five smaller groups of "friends."

Coach Dye called all the players together for a meeting the next day. He said only a few words: "You're not a team. If you want to win football games, don't leave this room until you are a team." And he and the other coaches left the room. As you can imagine, this dramatic gesture sparked a lot of conversation. I didn't have the language then, but looking back, we talked about alignment and helping each other by working and playing our positions well "together." When the players left later that day, we had all committed to being a team and to winning by playing our part as a whole and doing the best we could for our teammates first and ourselves second.

The next Saturday we played the Citadel, which had a formidable defense with an All-American middle linebacker. The game was the most intense and hardest hitting one I ever played in. We won 3-0. We finished that season with unexpected wins over the University of North Carolina and the University of Virginia, and won the conference championship the next season. The same collection of talent that lost games it was supposed to win won games it was expected to lose when the players became accountable to each other and, as a necessary corollary, to themselves.

Accountability to the Future

Holding yourself and asking and reminding your followers to hold themselves accountable might seem to cover the subject, but as we've seen, leaders have broader responsibility. They are accountable to the organization itself as future conditions shift and change, but also to immediate society and beyond. If leaders don't think about the future, the future may surprise them by becoming a hostile environment. To be prepared as best you can is extremely important. I have found the truly accountable look to the future and prepare—yet deal with their current duties. Being accountable to the organization means you have responsibility to the future in three ways, though they all work themselves out in the present, too.

Stay On-Purpose

First, you as leader must ensure that the direction and values remain viable, but also that everyone remains on-purpose, aligned with the organization's vision and its goals, and accountable to their roles in service of that purpose. Particularly in today's fast-changing environment, this can be a big challenge. Here's an example of a failure to meet it:

> The marketing director for a large Fortune 500 company had worked for years to identify the right market and hire the best business development people for his company. This market had fed the company well for years, but lately that market had changed, and the company needed to change as well if it was to continue to prosper. Consequently, the director set out to find a new market to "provide employment" for the business development people he had hired. He was going to refit them to the new situation to avoid tough choices about his employees.
>
> Though he was concerned about his people, he was not accountable to the mission of the enterprise. His first question should have been "what is on-purpose for our company now?" In other words, "what market do we want to be in?" His second should have been "do we have the right people?" Not "how can I save my people?" He was acting responsibly, but toward the people over the mission and enterprise, and so he was not holding himself accountable to his role.

Concern for followers may seem admirable, but if leaders are not accountable to their role, the purpose, and the future, then the organization itself may fail, thereby affecting many more people negatively.

Anticipating Gaps

Second, to be truly accountable to the organization, a leader must anticipate problems by projecting the company's activities into the future or reexamining current practices to discern where they could come up short or go wrong. Doing so helps position the organization for future success. We learn from mistakes, but leaders should see this, though often necessary, as a luxury. Better to anticipate errors and avoid them altogether. A good way to illustrate this point is in regard to safety. Holding yourself and others accountable for anticipating safety issues has a tremendous payoff.

Tim Gelbar notes that his company holds regular safety conferences to review and assess thinking and behavior, as well as statistics. After years of intensive development, he and his executives developed powerful guidelines for behavior that they hold themselves accountable to and that they believe will lead to even greater success. The company calls these "Do It Now" behaviors and has placed them onto small pocket cards that list various behaviors that enhance safety and remind employees how to act in different situations. The executive team reviews these at its meetings to see if its members have been acting with integrity. By the executives demonstrating these behaviors, they give employees permission to learn, grow, change their behavior, and hold each other accountable to these new expectations. Here is the list on the cards:

Do It Now Behaviors
1. When feeling certain, seek blind spots.
2. Discussing differing opinions is the first step toward alignment.
3. Seek help early; don't let your ego get in the way.
4. Marketing and Operations 'jump" together or not at all.
5. Learning from mistakes is not failure.
6. Seek purpose, not comfort.
7. First hold yourself accountable, then ask others to do the same.

Invisible Social Contracts (That Bind the Not-Accountable Leader)
Third, who is going to lead the organization in the future? My company has conducted more than thirty year-long, high-potential development programs for up-and-comers who their companies believe will be capable one day of leading at the executive level. During the selection process we use, the organization itself comes up with the criteria used to select individuals for the program. Usually these

Acting Accountably

criteria include two or three characteristics indicating potential for leadership. Early in my career, however, I noticed a peculiar pattern: the candidates the first year were not nearly as good as those in the second year and later rounds.

When I spotted this pattern, I asked a number of people why it occurred. The answer was always the same: people feel obligated to give a spot in this high-profile, high-potential training to the ones who have been the most loyal, not necessarily to those considered most competent to lead in the future. What I call "invisible social contracts" bound the executives, causing them to either be blind to the person's performance or more likely to not have the heart to pick a better alternative, and thus risk potential alienation and lack of followership. It takes courage to choose to be on-purpose and accountable, and risk alienation from those you depend on.

Next to hiring well, developing future leaders is one of the most important tasks an organization can undertake. Yet frequently organizations thwart it by playing favorites and not basing these decisions on what's good for the organization going forward. This kind of behavior comes at the expense of the future performance of the enterprise.

Advocacy and Alienation

As a survival response to a hostile environment, early man figured out that when others were "watching your back," you and your loved ones had a greater chance of survival. As human beings aged or became sick and unable to support themselves physically, without a community to support them, they would probably die. This same instinct to be a part of the group can be seen in organizations and on teams today. It is a blessing—but without awareness, it is also a curse to the leader holding him- or herself accountable to transforming an organization.

Social-psychological research has shown time and again that a fundamental human drive is to seek advocacy. In one study, researchers planted a hundred dollar bill for a subject to find while accompanied by a "stranger" (another person in the experimental cohort). Upon finding the money, the subject was asked how much he or she would give the stranger who just happened to be there. What the experimenters found was that the subjects' behavior is fairly predictable—the "finder" subject will often split the money fifty-fifty even though the subject is not obligated to do so. If there is the potential to see the person again, the frequency of sharing goes up even more. An unspoken social contract forms: "I have helped you, so I can expect you to come to my defense if necessary later."

This innate human tendency shows up in business. The more executive amplitude or "social power" the other person has (such as a CEO or senior executive) or wealth, the greater the potential "survival" value of the apparently selfless (but not actually selfless) act. This is the force that allows leaders to direct and focus the behavior of the people in the typical organization in our culture. In universities and other types of professional organizations, I've noticed over the years, this rather political approach to leadership is widely used. It is akin to the leader holding an air hose through which subordinates breathe underwater—do something I don't like, and I'll squeeze your hose slowly until it's closed; do what I want and I'll loosen my hold on it.

Can you envision it—cavemen and women scratching each other's backs, not realizing the basis of political behavior was forming? This deeply held belief in the unspoken social contract that mobilizes people to seek the perceived safety of advocacy is quite frustrating to real leaders trying to enact necessary transformation in an organization. Years ago in one company I dealt with, a midlevel executive was brought in to lead what he was told was a well-functioning department. Upon his arrival, the CEO welcomed him with a challenge: reduce a 4 million dollar shortfall—20–25 percent of the department's budget. The new executive had no time to develop the advocacy among his followers necessary to support that magnitude of change, but if he waited to act, the organization would go under. He immediately rationalized the numbers, studied the market, thought about all the possible ways to cut overhead, but all his thinking was to no avail. There was only one option: he had to cut salaries. Good intentions lay behind this act, but since he had developed no advocacy, he found no support, only resistance: the people in the group he took over saw him as the CEOs henchman in harming their interests. This

Acting Accountably

couldn't be further from the truth, but the first couple of years were a rough ride. The exec received hate mail, and he experienced the effects of nasty politics trying to preserve the past—even though the organization would have failed if he had not acted.

The Problem with Pleasing Behavior

The environment around us has changed from the days of cavemen and women. The pace of change has accelerated, and to survive in the kind of future that is fast approaching, leaders must see that advocacy is a behavioral trap. A real leader cannot take action without actual, often political, or at least perceived risk. "You scratch my back and I'll scratch yours"—this belief has been a great source of our success as a species and it's also a great source of effective team-oriented behavior, but without awareness, this belief is also a common reason human organizations fail. It's a way to kill real leadership. When it does, the organization experiences unnecessary and unintended negative outcomes.

The Japanese have a saying: "leaders are carried to the top of the organization on the backs of the people they help." This is in large part true, but also true is that without the acknowledgment and support of those in "power," for succession to take place, there must be a "revolution." Advocacy is essential if a person is to be successful in an organization; without the acknowledgment and support of those in power, the real leader will likely be ejected like a virus from the human body. The problem arises when higher leaders select and support only those leaders below them they fundamentally agree with—that process preserves the status quo. Nothing changes unless real leadership emerges.

Fear of Alienation

As we have seen, often leaders go against the grain in the organization, against the way it operated in the past. When this is true, it can be virtually impossible to get buy-in from both higher leaders and

63

subordinates to make significant changes in behavior, even in the face of impending failure. Many executives charged with change and facing resistance will use a "burning platform," forcing a crisis to scare people into changing—and this approach can work, at least at first. But the hard truth is that a real leader bringing about real transformation out of necessity will likely experience a cold shoulder from those he or she leads. No human being likes to feel alienated from the group, including leaders. However, this alienation is often associated with transformation. The leader who cannot handle this alienation is likely not a good person to lead change. It is difficult to keep an open mind and be vulnerable to those who would throw you under the bus to get things back to the status quo.

Leaders who cannot stomach alienation will often compromise so they can once again feel a part of the group. This compromising usually ends up in a regression to the mean, a return to past behavior. In one of our programs called "Leadership Decathlon®," where we work with usually younger high-potential managers and executives, we have a process whereby they anonymously interview senior executives. One of the questions they ask is this: "Is it lonely at the top?" Amazingly, about a third of the executives asked this question answer, "it isn't lonely." What I've discovered in exploring how the higher leaders respond to this question is that the more senior the executive, the lonelier that person feels. The stark reality is that the effective leader will have to make unpopular decisions. Stable-state managers likely do not feel as lonely.

Surfacing Misalignment with Accountability

In a transforming organization that lacks accountability, both measurable behavior and emotional dynamics will regress to the mean, to the behavior and the relationships that were normal in the old corporate culture. Without accountability, a leader can only grope in the dark as to why the organization is not achieving its goals. One of the benefits of a truly accountable system is that it often brings to light hidden misalignment with the purpose on the part of those who espouse head, heart, and behavioral alignment but who are not really in alignment. The last things these individuals want is to have clear accountability in place. They cannot espouse alignment but not act in alignment and stay hidden from view.

This is why some alienation will occur when the executive first sets up his or her system of accurate reporting with goals and clear expectations with time limits. The leader who can stomach this alienation is moving through the quit zone toward the jumping point, bringing about Senge's creative tension. The leader who can keep moving, communicating clearly and effectively and maintaining consistent accountability, is getting ready to jump. If the leader does, some followers who at first are alienated will come along. They will move into alignment, and they'll become more comfortable with accountability. Some may not. Accountability will tell the leader who they are and how they are misaligned. The real leader then faces the opportunity to enable them to move into alignment, or else to move on if they can't, or won't.

Courage and Compromise

It's clear that real leaders need one trait especially: courage. It's the distinguishing aspect of accountability. The discussion earlier on developing future leadership shows why the opposite aspect of courage is compromise. We typically see compromise as a virtue. It can be one within personal relationships and in politics, where persons or parties need to give some to reach mutual agreement for the purpose of societal governance. In leading organizations to change, though, compromise usually means retaining some of the habitual behavior of the past and avoiding some of the necessary behavior for the future. "Outside influences, seniors in the company, markets, etc. can bring pressures to bear in which compromise or feigned ignorance is more comfortable and acceptable but which drives compromises that are hard to back away from or undo," said one executive. Compromise in organizations usually arises when courage is lacking.

The leader has to be the first to jump out into the quit zone and move through it, and doing so takes courage. Many leaders will talk about change and camp out on the cliff's rim, and even con themselves into believing they're leading change, but they don't jump. They and their followers will deploy the familiar rationalizations of the corpocentric defense mechanisms—compromise, to avoid jumping.

One role of a leader is to chart the organization's direction. Real leaders seek information and opinions from followers; they ask followers to help figure out how the organization can get from where it is to where they all want it to go. But as a leader, you need to make the important final decisions, then communicate them and what implementing them will entail down to the members of your team. Once you do, you then encourage followers to make suggestions for actions to improve the course, and facilitate the process for such suggestions. A real leader, though, makes the tough decisions. They're tough because they often go against the grain of the organization's habitual behavior—but they must be made if the organization is to change and achieve its mission. Making them requires courage; you have to be the first to jump off of the cliff.

When you do, you find that courage is contagious. A leader who consistently seeks information and suggestions but then makes tough decisions that are in the best interest of the organization inspires confidence in his or her followers. This confidence gives the followers a sense of security. It helps them decide to make the jump themselves.

The Abdication Curve and Leadership Lag

Leaders seeking to maintain accountability to the company's purpose and the accountability of themselves and their followers to that purpose need to beware of a major obstacle that often looms in organizations. Consider these scenarios:

A physician leading a large unit wants a perfect solution and holds endless debates without any action—and eventually the department has to lay off twenty people.

Acting Accountably

A new client tells a sales rep that he wants to send someone to a program the company holds, and the request gets lost in a shuffle of paper—and the client goes to a competitor down the street.

An executive team does strategic planning, but gets too busy to follow through with tough decisions with the execution plan, so the company eventually goes broke and is bought by a private equity firm for "pennies on the dollar."

An executive fears giving accurate, timely, and useful performance feedback to a key subordinate and so doesn't—and the subordinate's unit eventually fails and the executive is fired.

What do these incidents have in common? They reflect a failure to be accountable or to hold others accountable to their role, causing something known as "leadership lag." Jim Farr developed a model by this name in his book *Supraconscious Leadership*; I've adapted it over the years, but the basic concept is the same as his:

> *Leadership lag is the time it takes an individual leader or organization to identify an issue or opportunity and take successful action on it. When a leader waits too long to take action or when a leader takes thoughtless action, the result is increased potential for a negative unintended outcome—more expensive and sometimes catastrophic.*

Leaders need to be on the alert for leadership lag so they can catch it early. Leadership lag causes loss and it wastes talent, time, and resources. Recognizing leadership lag can be difficult because it springs from old beliefs and habitual behavior that lie below the level of consciousness until one is self-aware. The leadership lag model is an analytical discussion tool for project teams and organizational leaders to help them become aware of organizational habitual behavior before the negative effects of leadership lag strike (see figure 3).

Figure 3. Organizational Entropy: Leadership Lag

Genichi Taguchi's loss functions theory includes the concept of "optimization," whereby one can find an optimal approach and timing in response to a given situation, and implies a right balance—not too much or too little of something relating to a particular function. This sense indicates why acting too quickly can cause leadership lag as easily as waiting too long to act—the results of that action may need to be undone, resulting in waste of resources and lost time.

The "abdication curve" in figure 3 goes up as denial occurs in the awareness stage (which can lead to acting too quickly as well as avoiding action), analysis paralysis occurs in the alignment stage where decisions are made, and compromise occurs in the action and accountability stage. The greater the curve, the more loss and waste there is, and the greater the chance of catastrophic loss. Conversely, the straighter the line, which when curved represents abdication, the lower the loss and waste.

Three Phases
Three key phases (functions, in the Taguchi sense) of human leadership where we need to be aware of leadership lag are:

Acting Accountably
1. Seeing an issue, risk, or opportunity.
2. Analyzing, and aligning decision with purpose and with others.
3. Taking right accountable action.

Working at the optimal rate of speed through these phases is critical to the success of leaders, projects, and organizations. After years of working with leaders and their organizations, I believe it is one of the key differences between a great organization, project, or leader and those that are not reaching their potential. To succeed, to reach optimal performance, leaders must systematically, often incrementally reduce leadership lag.

Expanding Awareness to See an Issue or Opportunity

Information flow is the first and the fundamental requirement in reducing leadership lag. If it is of poor quality (scant or inaccurate) or not timely enough, then the decision-making process is hampered. Ensuring an accurate and timely flow is not easy. Both personal and organizational barriers often stop or slow the flow of information and thereby make timely and accurate decision making harder. The pressure that deadlines create and the resistance that ego defense mechanisms produce will work against high-quality information flow.

For instance, you can be quite embarrassed if you don't meet an agreed-on deadline with a boss, colleague, or client who relies on you for the success of the project. Many talented service providers will work long hours to try to meet the deadline and will avoid telling the other they are running behind until it is too late. Ironically, the very people the provider is trying to insulate from the problem causing the delay usually have the most to offer (information and informed judgment) to alter the problem's negative impact. Better to feel the embarrassment, talk early, and get the help you need.

Breaking the strong, ingrained personal and cultural habits in an organization requires a leader to give people *permission to do what's right*. This includes permission to speak openly and early. You as leader must make sure all your subordinates and their followers know that you expect information that is as accurate as possible in order for you and the rest of your team to assess a situation as clearly as possible and base decisions on real conditions, not habitual perceptions based on automated behavior and corporate culture. People need to know clearly that they are expected to help each other as well.

The mentality that typically motivates action in organizations and that you will have to confront can be buried deep in the unconscious mind, reinforced by the corporate culture. For example, suppose a client wants to be closely involved in planning and work on a project, but your company's provider has absorbed repeatedly over years the notion that "I know my job is to take care of routine problems and not bother the client with them." The potential for a troubled relationship is high. Thus the importance of making clear the expectations for accurate and timely information flow, encouraging people to speak, and emphasizing they should ask for help.

Most of the time, people will not believe you when you give permission to speak and do what's right until there is a failure that you can use to teach this point. Let's hope it's a small one. Let's hope it comes early.

Helping someone is easy, but asking for help is hard, because of the ego defenses. Often when someone who has trouble getting past those defenses does ask for help, it's too late—sometimes catastrophically so.

Seeking to Align Decision with Purpose

Once accurate information is flowing with speed, the leader or team needs to determine the right course of action. Even with good information, though, leaders can develop leadership lag in this phase. Most often, it happens because of two opposite behavioral types, who illustrate the twin prongs of leadership lag.

The Overthinker: This type of leader uses the decision-making process as a way to avoid taking action. This is analysis paralysis; leaders paralyzed by analysis request more and more information, then overthink and overdiscuss but never leave this second phase and enter the action phase—their subconscious's way of avoiding the risk of failure. Ironically, this behavior moves these leaders and those being led toward the failure they fear. Eventually they may end up being seen as stupid and incompetent—which they are not, and which

70

is exactly what they were afraid of experiencing in the first place. *Overthinkers* are the campers on the edge of the cliff in the quit zone. They talk about jumping, but they never jump. The result of their inaction is leadership lag.

The Action Cowboy: This type of leader, propelled by a need to get the job done, effectively skips over the second phase and jumps right into action without taking time to prioritize the relative importance of a decision or to analyze the situation based on information that's available. The cowboy thus ends up wasting time on less important matters, leaving little time for concentrating on the important ones. A variation of this type is too busy to focus, wanting to be helpful and getting too many balls in the air—and ending up dropping them. Action cowboys don't take the time to understand the issue, align their decisions with the mission and values of the organization, and anticipate problems. Driven to check off the box and achieve, they slow their teams down in the long run, creating leadership lag.

What an organization needs is not an overthinker or an action cowboy but an *optimizer*. Finding the right balance of information and analysis to determine an effective course of action is hard to do alone. An optimizer ensures that the right people are at the table, those with the requisite expertise and knowledge to solve the problems at hand—including executives, customer reps, and customers. They don't fear what Robert Quinn calls "Building the Bridge as You Walk on It." The optimizer also discerns when it's time to move. Though experts may have good information and be willing to voice strong opinions, they may be afraid to decide by themselves in a timely manner. The optimizer needs to know when to ask, "Do we have enough information to decide?" The optimizer reduces leadership lag.

Taking Right Accountable Action

When the leader has decided on the right course of action, holding people accountable for its achievement takes skill and courage, especially when that leader is changing an existing system or process and the associated human behavior. Transforming an organization to respond with agility to new conditions in the market and the world at large means orienting toward a refined purpose and often new goals, and as we have seen in that regard, doing so requires new values and beliefs and new behavior. To achieve them, an organization must have clarity of understanding of the new targets (see Lencioni 2012), and regular, systematic communication about the purpose, the goals, and the beliefs and behavior and honest feedback about performance and changing conditions.

But usually when a company undertakes this kind of transformation, inertia, fear, anger, and political battling associated with old work habits stabilized by years of repetition arise. Disrupting the deep sleep of familiar behavioral work patterns usually provokes resistance of some sort by "good people with old habits." An executive team may have carefully fashioned a plan of action that seems to the members of the team a great idea, but to a subcontractor who has worked for years in a certain way, this new idea may pose a huge challenge. That subcontractor is going to need support. Holding not only others but yourself accountable to the purpose in the face of tenacious reluctance to change old habits is tough work, and often, as we saw in regard to alienation, it is lonely work.

Here's an example I witnessed of what can happen when a leader risks alienation in transforming an organization and runs into politics:

A few years ago, in anticipation of changes in health care (e.g., bundling insurance payments into one lump sum whereby internal practices have to negotiate their share instead of each subspecialty getting paid directly by the insurance company), a newly hired physician executive of a private hospital moved into leadership mode and was the first to begin to make significant changes in the way the medical and administrative staff worked and was paid. The changes caused fear on the part of many of those who reported to him, and they went around him to longtime friends and colleagues in the organization's leadership beside and above him to complain. Surprisingly, his peers had difficulty in supporting his leadership. They had built relationships over years, the invisible social contracts I mentioned earlier, that they found hard to break. Politics, although necessary in organizations, can also cause the wrong things to be done for the wrong reasons.

The new executive stayed on high ground. He committed no ethical violations. He never bad-mouthed anyone. In fact, he was trying to retain as many people on the staff as possible. As politically connected subordinates continued to vent about his leadership to their friends in high places, these leaders found it harder and harder to support the changes. They didn't have the stomach for the difficult but necessary leadership required to reinforce what everyone knew conceptually was essential change. They had never had to really lead before.

If it hadn't been for the CEO, other leadership in the organization would have ejected the executive and the hospital would have returned to the status quo—resulting in potentially catastrophic loss through leadership lag and thus resulting in much greater organizational pain down the road. Benjamin Franklin's well-known axiom "a stitch in time saves nine" is instructive.

Many of those complaining had threatened to quit if the CEO went forward and supported the executive, but most didn't. Well-intended but misguided, habitual leadership would have thrown more people under the bus in the long run by not supporting the executive, but the CEO had the stomach for real leadership and made the unpopular decision to support the new initiative and the executive leading it. The CEO had jumped earlier, before he hired the executive. Not because he wanted to, but he felt he had to as part of his duty for sound management and because he had a willingness to sacrifice popularity for a shot at the right outcome. He stayed "on-purpose." In the long run it worked out much better, and the hospital is now positioned for success ahead of many of its competitors.

Just as with the thinking and deciding phase, the action phase is marked by some leadership tendencies that increase leadership lag.

Leadership Beyond Belief

The Planner: These people love to conceptualize, to design and plan initiatives. They often assume, wrongly, that people will follow through on what was agreed to in the planning session without systematic detailed follow-up. When initiatives fail, planners see the solution as requiring more thinking and planning. I've seen their offices walled with notebook after notebook of failed systems and processes that were brilliantly designed but never fully implemented. Often, the conceptualizer is creative, spotting issues early, but gets bored after the planning, moving from one item to another on a list, too distracted to complete work on any of them. Clearly, conceptualizers will find maintaining accountability difficult. If they don't become aware of their tendencies and learn how to prioritize, they will need a complementary partner who's good at that task, or their projects and sometimes their careers may die in the doldrums of implementation.

The Pleaser: We will see more about pleasers in chapter 7. They don't have the stomach to hold people accountable for the changes needed. In a transformational initiative, they tend to think they can get others to work hard and implement change for them because they are liked. They tend to delude themselves. They *are* usually well liked, but they're not always respected. Because they are often overly empathic and compassionate, they find being around others in pain and frustration difficult. They often don't give accurate, useful feedback or timely performance reviews; as a result, their subordinates often don't know they are failing until it is too late. The pleaser then ends up taking the blame.

The Chainsaw: After an organization experiences years of cumulative compromise or excessive leadership lag, it usually has to bring in an executive to fix the mess. Generally, such an organization is characterized by political entrenchment and has an executive team that doesn't have the stomach for necessary change, as seen in the hospital mentioned above (if the CEO hadn't been a real leader, that is). The chainsaw is goal driven and often makes decisions based almost completely on financial considerations. Chainsaws usually don't have much feeling, or if they do, they don't show it. They certainly don't show much compassion or any empathy for employees going through change. These leaders are often successful turnaround artists, but once the turnaround is accomplished, they must leave, because employees will not sustain motivation on their behalf in the long term.

Some executives learn to do both stable-state management and turnaround, but they are few and far between. A company is much better off with a stable-state manager who continually works to optimize information flow, decision making, and accountable action and reduce the organization's leadership lag—in other words, a real leader—so that bringing in a chainsaw is not necessary.

Reducing Leadership Lag

What can you as a leader motivated to lead a transformational process to align your company with its purpose and reach new goals do to reduce leadership lag and increase accountability? Here are a few suggestions:

1. Take each of the three phases above and ask yourself and your associates: where is our greatest weakness—seeing, deciding, or taking action? Once there is agreement hold an in-depth discussion of "what do we need to *continue* doing, what do we need to *stop* doing, and what do we need to *start* doing to optimize our processes and reduce leadership lag?"

2. Build a common language and model of leadership in your project or company. Send your leaders to a self-awareness-based leadership development program. My firm runs one each month, and there are other good ones too.

3. Make "leadership lag" a term you use regularly in debriefing project assignments as well as in your performance reviews. Ask for ways to improve performance to make better decisions more rapidly.

4. Track your organization's performance in meeting deadlines and objectives. One way to do this is to set up an "initiatives log" or what we call a "Path Forward" (figure 4), where days late on project promises are documented. Use this as a part of your performance appraisal process. See if you can improve performance and reward better performance.

Leadership Beyond Belief

5. Practice thoughtful delegation to give yourself a "time payment" and effectively give people a chance to grab empowerment in effective ways. Use the approach outlined in appendix 4 for six months.

Action Item	Point Person	Others Responsible	By When	Status	Date Initiated	Initiated By
Organize and distribute notes to the team	Sandra	Frankie	14 Nov 16	C	6 Nov 16	Team
Set monthly meeting dates to follow up on objectives	Sandra	Frankie	14 Nov 16	C	6 Nov 16	
Efficient effective processes (financial) plan submitted to Frankie	Susan	Mark	14 Nov 16	A	6 Nov 16	
All jobs are profitable; goals are clear and exceeded	Autumn	Rich	14 Nov 16	B	6 Nov 16	
Efficient effective business processes used with discipline	Sandra	Frankie	14 Nov 16	A	6 Nov 16	
Final integrated business plan achieved	Frankie	Mark	31 Dec 16	A	6 Nov 16	

Figure 4. Path Forward (Excel Spreadsheet Used to Help Hold Accountability on Teams)

Do not scold when followers bring issues to the table. Encourage them to solve them at the lower levels, but to come sooner if they are going to miss a date that will hurt a partner. By doing so, you are giving permission to decrease leadership lag. If they continue to bring issues without being able to resolve them or miss deadlines without communicating or seeking help, you may need to try scolding once, and if that doesn't work, give them a promotion to another project or company.

Jumping into the Unknown

Clearly, real leadership that demands accountability takes courage to face the kind of resistance and other obstacles we've seen in this chapter. But it takes a different kind of courage as well. As a leader of a transformation, you are holding yourself and others accountable for results, but you have only a probability of success, not a guarantee. Even if everyone maintains integrity, alignment, and accountability, though success is more likely, failure is still possible. This looming threat creates another type of fear besides the discomfort provoked by changing habitual behavior. Most people are afraid of venturing into the unknown.

Accountability involves the ability to stomach that fear and the uncertainty, as well as the discomfort that comes from breaking free of habit, until the excitement and awareness of Senge's "creative tension," mentioned in chapter 4, sets in. Accountability to the organization's purpose means leading self and others in an endeavor that, after all, is somewhat irrational—believing in a future that doesn't exist but is desired, one that will require new beliefs and unproven behavior to achieve. Real leadership is jumping off the cliff of established beliefs and tested behavior into the abyss of uncertainty.

This point is the edge of the cliff of the quit zone, where many turn back to remain stuck in the feeling of certainty of past belief, behavior, and memory—often to the demise of their personal satisfaction in life and, for leaders, the organization they are responsible to.

Making this jump is true transformation and it is what distinguishes a great leader from a politician or manager.

Act Accountably

If you believe your unit or team or organization is weak in acting accountably, here are some recommendations.

1. Develop goals and metrics to follow key indicators of success. The "balanced scorecard" is a good approach to use as well as creating simple (but not simplistic) dashboards of lead and lag measures of success. Make sure you have "touchpoints" that let you know when things are heading in the wrong direction.

2. Assess the readiness of someone you are giving a challenging assignment. Make sure they are to hold themselves accountable to their role and the task at hand. Adjust your follow-up and reporting in against that person's experience and demonstrated performance. Lengthen and loosen this as he or she demonstrates competency over time. Make it clear that "touchpoints" and "reporting" are not micromanaging.

3. Make sure to hold a conversation with those you delegate to, finding out if they have the resources to be truly "response-able." Remember, your "executive amplitude" may make it difficult for some to admit they don't have the resources. Make sure they tell you the truth and then negotiate from there. Once response-able, they can then be held account-able.

4. Maybe the most important factor is immediate feedback to someone when he or she is not reaching agreed-to targets in the agreed-to time frames. Compromising only enhances organizational entropy. Have the courage to avoid leadership lag. A good way is to talk in terms of "on-purpose" and "off-purpose" behavior or actions. This depersonalizes the

feedback and if used well reflects accurately who is accountable.

5. Read chapter 8, which will give you an ABCs of performance feedback, before giving your annual feedback to the people who report to you.

6. Hold an in-depth and honest conversation with the management team about "leadership lag" and where your organization is weak in the see, decide, and act continuum. Where do you tend to abdicate your responsibility? What does the organization tolerate?

7. During or after each meeting make sure to populate and update your "Path Forward." Check back in at each meeting to see who is keeping his or her time frame and performance agreements and who is not. If someone breaks a time frame, counsel that person in private and make sure he or she gives you a workaround. If after two or three times missing deadlines, put the person on a ninety-day plan. Make sure to use the situation to ensure the person understands that *he* is accountable for his performance.

Chapter 4
Seek Alignment (with Purpose, Self, and Others)
Integrity or Hypocrisy in Leadership

Although invisible to many, companies operate by beliefs and customary behavior, just as individuals do. Becoming aware in a corporate context means uncovering those beliefs and the resulting automated behavior that no longer serve the new, changed direction, mission, or purpose. Just as a person's identity reflects the ego he or she has formed, and just as that ego generates defenses, a company or organization projects an identity, and it generates defenses, which I call "corpocentrism." As you read earlier, corporate patterns of behavior become entrenched and handed down. When a company sails into uncharted water with unfamiliar weather patterns, the same beliefs and behaviors that contributed to former success, if unexamined, changed, or consciously limited, could cause it to run aground.

If you can recognize the controlling beliefs and the resulting automated behavior within the organization, then you gain the power, just as you do in your own life, to choose the organization's *future* beliefs and values, to choose the new aligned behavior that will cause it to thrive in today's business and social environment—and tomorrow's. However, awareness of old patterns of belief and behavior is

Seek Alignment

only the starting point. Aligning, focusing, and realigning mind-sets, beliefs, and behavior around a common purpose is the next step.

Alignment requires first determining what is right for the organization, based on its purpose now and in a projected future, including goals, the strategy for attaining them, and the company's core values. Organizational self-examination—of its purpose, anchored in those core values—provides a vision of where the organization should go. That vision will guide you as you align the organization, peers and followers, and yourself with the purpose and new behavior so that the business can fulfill that purpose.

Alignment within the Self

Naive leaders ask themselves this question: "How can I get individuals to do what I need them to do?" This question is off the mark. Real leaders fundamentally see the leader-follower relationship differently and thereby phrase this essential question differently: "How do I determine what behavior on my part will cause my followers to motivate themselves to do what I need them to do?" If you as a leader are to find an answer that works, you have to perform the art of "causing followership." Learning this art begins with realizing a simple truth: no leader can achieve his or her goals without the efforts of others. And the key is to truly understand that the follower supplies the energy for achieving an outcome.

This is not semantics and has very significant implications and makes a huge difference—in your life and for the organization. If you think you are the source of the energy and motivation for others, you will likely face a future of burnout and the inability to provide the direction for your group, as you will be mired in attempting to "motivate" others. With this wrong perspective, you will at some point become limited in the scope of leadership you can handle without making yourself miserable. This fundamental and incredibly important shift in perspective raises a question: do you want to create dependents requiring your help and energy or strong adults taking on responsibility and getting the monkey off your back? If you desire the latter, it is important that you take the insight from this chapter

81

seriously. Fundamentally, this shift will require subtle perception, and mastering the art of causing followership. Doing so requires both self-awareness and awareness of what drives other people.

Hypocrisy in Self-Alignment

Alignment raises two opposing characteristics: hypocrisy and integrity. Both involve the ordinary sense of those words, but both also have special meanings in the context of alignment. Awareness, as we will see in chapter 7, means seeing clearly. One of the primary aids to seeing clearly within an organization is communication, including listening, encouraging transparency, and seeking feedback. Full alignment requires a regular flow of information between people so they can come to common understandings and resolve misalignment issues. Leaders who genuinely want to align must not only place a high value on communication but must actively practice and seek to enhance it. Communication from below does not generally occur on its own at the rate a leader needs in order to make well-informed decisions. Leaders must intentionally channel the flow of information. In many organizations, they don't.

Frequently, leaders make decisions on partial information, and seek information that confirms their beliefs. This attitude causes serious problems. John Allison, former CEO of BB&T, has said that the greatest factor behind large mistakes business leaders make is failing to pay attention to information received that contradicts a belief such leaders hold about themselves or about the world. Such resistance to information that challenges those beliefs leads to failure in those leaders' decisions ("John Allison" 2011).

Information Flow—the Lifeblood of Organizations

In organizations today, a constant flow of accurate information is often disrupted by bad systems, bad relationships, blind spots, or office politics. While often uncomfortable to most executives and managers who seek approval, the most valuable kind of information from followers is constructive negative feedback. Any leader who protects his or her fragile ego by appearing perfect, strong, or all-knowing will stop this vital flow of information. Most importantly, this feedback tells leaders where they have missed the mark in the process of aligning followers' needs with their goals and purpose (a blind spot).

As we will see in chapter 7 and the Johari Window model, the ego carries out defensive action when the identity's image is threatened, and so the natural reaction is to resist hearing negative feedback. Most managers want feedback about their operations in the form of numerical data; most don't get—and most don't want—explicit feedback on their leadership. In avoiding such qualitative feedback, managers isolate themselves. They also set a norm, with their actions emulated by others, that says "open and honest information is not tolerated when it hurts ego." When they, often inadvertently, send this message, negative consequences that were avoidable surprise them and then create unintended negative consequences neither they nor anyone else wants. We may undervalue perceptual and opinion-based feedback, but it reflects the mind-sets and beliefs of those being led and, thus, is very significant and should be effectively addressed.

It may not seem like it, but this avoidance of feedback constitutes a type of hypocrisy: if leaders express a desire—even to themselves—to become aware and see clearly in order to align their followers and the organization, and if communication is vital for seeing clearly, then shutting off feedback is a hypocritical action.

Don't underestimate the difficulty of a leader's receiving honest feedback. This is why actively seeking to promote communication is so important. A formula (from Farr and Grinnell 2009) about business and other organizations that all leaders should keep at the forefront of their minds is this:

> *The higher a leader is in an organizational hierarchy, the lower the quality of information that leader will receive.*

In your effort to be truly aware, you need to realize a blunt truth: if you are at the executive level, you rarely get valuable feedback about your leadership. Subordinates' natural tendency is to curry favor with the highest leaders, which deprives the leader of feedback about his or her shortcomings. The higher the position, power, and scope of responsibility a leader holds, the bigger the problem of inadequate information flow becomes. You may get feedback, but it's not the right kind: a CEO is much more likely to have his or her ego groomed with supportive information than is the janitor. To see clearly, you don't need supportive information (i.e., flattery that doesn't tell you anything important); you need accurate, timely, and useful information.

The four worst reactions of a leader to feedback are these:

1.   Discounting or defending his or her position.
2.   Devaluing or ignoring the information.
3.   Attacking the messenger.
4.   Believing the information without obtaining more data (from multiple sources).

When you respond in any of these ways, you communicate to the person giving the feedback (and to anyone else he or she may tell about the incident) that input is not valued. Or that you "shoot from the hip" and are not reliable as a leader. As a consequence, you will put a stop to the flow of valuable information of any sort from that source (and possibly from others).

You cannot respond effectively to current conditions without accurate information. It is the basis on which an organization makes effective decisions, plans, and schedules. A genius with an IQ of 155 may be terrific at analyzing situations before making decisions, but that person will make poorer decisions than an ordinary person with a normal but lower IQ who has better information. That ordinary person, if he or she works to maintain a flow of accurate information from below, is going to be a more effective leader than the genius who avoids it.

Failing to "Walk the Talk"

Leaders' alignment of their own actions with their followers' needs requires awareness and behavioral agility. Many executives speak about "walking the talk"—as long as walking doesn't rock the boat. Real leaders who perceive the needs of their followers respond to them with appropriate action, which means not only understanding

84

those needs but consciously adapting their own behavior to take them into account. Followers fully realize when leaders make the effort to understand what employees want and need, and when leaders act in ways that show they are part of the same team, and work toward the same goal. And everyone on that team realizes equally well when leaders do not. Once followers know you understand their views, and have considered them with openness and transparency, they will usually go along even if you don't accede to their requests.

If a leader understands what change is necessary and demands it from his or her followers, but isn't willing to change personally, followers will perceive this as hypocrisy, and will be unlikely to commit to the change and the goals. Most people, in fact, who have worked in companies or other types of organizations have likely experienced initiatives where processes were supposedly going to change, but observed that executive management did not behave any differently. Such experience breeds cynicism and resistance.

Over the years, I have noticed that organizations with open channels of communication and relatively authentic people respond to challenges better; organizations that restrict the flow of information, particularly any that disrupts the status quo, are less likely to respond effectively to the demands of the market or a complex project. Indeed, some executives will go to extreme measures to block information flow and avoid bad news:

Years ago I worked with a company president who seemed to be a great client. When we gave feedback to his executive team, he was very supportive, providing excellent leadership. We worked with his executives, one by one, on assessments and coaching for almost two years. At the end of the two years, we planned to perform an organizational climate study, to which the president agreed. At some point, though, he figured out that within this process he would receive feedback on his leadership, too. The process stopped and he discontinued the work. Looking back, I realized that over the years I'd had to be extremely sensitive in giving him even mildly critical feedback, which hinted that his personal fear and leadership were the cause of a problem.

In this case, too, a leader could fully intend to follow new behavior he or she sees as necessary to alignment, but failure to follow through is a hypocritical act and will limit the impact of changes.

Integrity in Self-Alignment

The key to encouraging a flow of accurate information from below to enable you to make better decisions is self-awareness. When you are armed with the self-awareness that enables you to step beyond the ego's defenses, you can listen to feedback without resisting. Some feedback may be painful to your ego to hear, but real leaders expand beyond the pain, realizing it is temporary and wanting to see clearly, and listen for any valuable information. I call this learned ability to listen beyond ego reactions as "growing your bowl"—that is, expanding your capacity for having normal human defensive reactions (when ego-identity is threatened) and still maintaining perspective to be on-purpose. I have developed a basic definition of feedback that may help place it in perspective:

> *Feedback is information about the state of an operation, behavior, or relationship—neither positive nor negative in itself, only in how it is interpreted.*

Showing subordinates that you value honest feedback about your actions leads them to trust you and to share more personal, valuable information about processes and operations in the organization. Remember, you won't hear bad things about your company unless you ask. It's easy to get good news, but you have to dig deep to get the bad, which is often the most useful.

An effective way to consider negative feedback, and one that helps deactivate ego defenses and reduces the desire to avoid the feedback, is to reframe it. Think of negative feedback as a reflection of the follower's perception based on his or her beliefs. When you consider it from this angle, it tends to lose much of its sting and becomes simply data you can use to give you a more complete picture of conditions and how your followers are reacting to them. A person's criticism, for example, can tell you more about that person's mind and how the person prioritizes goals than it does about your performance. Operating from this perspective is truly "mind reading." Since hearing criticism and interpreting the thinking behind it helps you discern that follower's needs, it provides valuable information indeed.

Walk a Mile in My Shoes

Agility, as pointed out earlier, is a necessity in order for an organization to adapt to changing conditions. Self-awareness is the basis of perceptual agility, which develops when you learn and practice the skill of listening and thinking outside your own frame of reference. You learn to see the world as others see it. If you work only from within your own frame of reference, you will severely limit your ability to accurately read your followers' needs. This skill grows from awareness, and noticing what drives other people—their values, beliefs, emotions, passions, fears, satisfactions, and desires.

> *If you tell me you don't like the shirt I am wearing, does that tell me more about my shirt or about your mind and how it perceives my shirt?*

This perceptual agility is valuable not only in providing insight into what will cause followers to motivate themselves to achieve the new purpose of an organization but also in providing a larger set of perceptions. Even a highly intelligent executive with excellent analytical ability has a limited perspective and can still learn from the perceptions of others. The best leaders, I have noticed over the years, share one characteristic: they have a desire to gain perspective in order to see reality clearly. Business visionary Tom Peters regularly hammers away at how important listening is. In fact, a video within his "Little Big Things" series, which you can find on his website, expresses it beautifully. The most effective executives know that taking the time to understand, listen, and then think about an issue or situation or challenge in order to put it in perspective is crucial for avoiding as many blunders as possible. Instead of immediately taking a position in a discussion or negotiation, they first seek others' points of view.

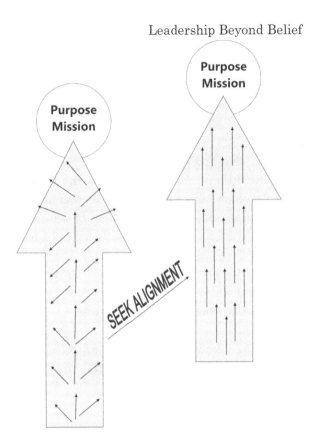

Figure 5. Alignment of Purpose-Goal and Needs (Based on Ideas in Senge 1990). Arrows depict individuals and their individual alignment, intent, and motivation within their unit or enterprise. Which one does your organization resemble?

Suspending Belief to Find Alignment

Peter Senge in *The Fifth Discipline* discusses the notion of "suspending belief," which helps us escape from the limited point of view we have created based on our personality. Recognizing that, if we continue to think and feel as we always have, we'll find only the solutions we have in the past, we consciously put our point of view, opinions, and emotions on hold in order to take a look at the perspective someone else has arrived at based on *his or her* beliefs. When we hold strong opinions, we tend to experience strong emotions associated with them, so suspending belief in those cases is difficult; the ego perceives a contrary opinion as a threat.

Suspending belief is the basis of finding more on-purpose alignment with the direction of the organization and, equally significant, a way to find greater collaborative alignment with those you work with (figure 5). It requires you to recognize that your opinion grew out of your beliefs and perceptions, and to step back and consciously try to view the issue from the other person's perspective; you may find that you have something to learn. Stepping outside your ego's boundaries and into uncertainty can cause anxiety, which Senge calls "creative tension" in this context. If you find your body rising in revolt, ride the dragon, and become curious.

Curiosity: The Basis of Listening

Frequently I have had Twitter conversations with Tom Peters (@tom_peters). His most famous book, *In Search of Excellence*, is a classic. In an exchange about the idea of "curiosity," he tweeted this definition: "By curiosity I mean deep engagement with you through which I learn." From our conversation, I could tell that he does not think he knows everything and is constantly open to learning. That I believe is his greatest strength—learning. This definition is a great expression of the meaning of learning. To put it into practice in a business setting (or in many other settings as well), I would phrase it this way:

> *Listen to one person today with whom you usually disagree and work to deeply understand the logic of that person's opinion.*

When we listen to people with an open, nonjudgmental mind, we gain their trust, respect, and support. Curiosity is thus a key to creating trusting relationships between colleagues, and between leaders and followers. It is an effective tool for countering the deployment of ego defenses.

Listening to someone you disagree with also effectively enhances communication. If you think about a person you really don't like to work with, who makes you uncomfortable, then I'd be willing to bet the flow of information between the two of you is choked off compared to the flow between you and someone you enjoy working with. Listening to the first person and demonstrating curiosity in what he or she thinks and why can sometimes bring you information you otherwise wouldn't receive.

Here's a way I express this thought to make it vivid:

We will listen to the advice of a trusted fool, and ignore the input of a distrusted genius.

Behaving in Alignment

A prerequisite for causing followership is a leader's taking action to align his or her own behavior with what is right for the organization as determined by a vision of the future, strategy, and core values, a vision developing out of work in awareness, of self and of the organization. When leaders change their own behavior to align with the organization's purpose and goals, followers have permission, so to speak, to change their own behavior—they are encouraged to do so by the example of the leader. In other words, the leader has to take the leadership jump first: mentally, behaviorally, and emotionally (see figure 6). Leaders must be all in or others will not follow fully, and again will talk and even walk a good game, but not be emotionally supportive. When the going gets tough, these followers will bail out through compromise and not hold themselves or others accountable.

Here is a personal example of aligning behavior based on a vision of necessary change:

I am now over sixty years old; even though I am fortunate to have energy and health, I know that I will not be able to keep up my current pace of consulting work when I am seventy. I have become aware that I am going to have to reconfigure my firm to let younger, talented people do the heavy lifting. To do so, I am going to have to risk my identity once more as I delegate key client relationships to others.

Leaders Close the Gap

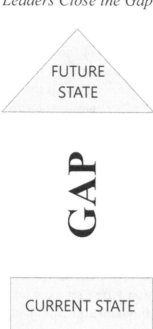

Figure 6. John Tarpey's Leadership Model

I'm going to have to work beyond the fantasy based on the false belief (due to my family history) that my worth is tied to my entrepreneurial and business success.

Making the changes necessary to achieve a new purpose will require those younger people to change how they behave in the firm as well. With a vision of more independence and authority, they can become energized to take on increased leadership. If I don't succeed in changing my own behavior, and continue to assume most of the responsibility and authority, they will become disillusioned and lose the motivation to change. So if I don't respond to this new challenge, I am going to be a very unhappy seventy-year-old. Writing this book is part of the plan. What feels secure now (the status quo) when looking ahead is actually more risky for me. Even though I feel the opposite—that safety lies in not changing. I know change is essential for me to realize the future I want.

When you as a leader are aware of the challenges that lie ahead and know precisely what road you need to go down, you face the choice of acting with integrity in conjunction with the values and purpose you wish to experience or espousing change yet acting hypocritically.

Alignment with Followers

While beliefs undergird habitual behavior and cause the automated actions that keep people from realizing their potential, the relationship is not necessarily negative. In the work of alignment with followers, you can take advantage of how beliefs cause behavior. Contrary to popular opinion, human beings act quite logically, using a certain type of thinking Jim Farr first mentioned to me, which we can call "psycho-logic." The fundamental rule (logic) behind this particular kind of acting is this:

> *People are reflexive; given a similar set of circumstances, people will think, act, and respond in the same ways over and over again.*

Once humans learn something through one trial learning or through repetition—as we saw with the Inuit visitor—they habituate, then automate, forming a belief that drives their perception and behavior from that point.

For instance, when you learn how to drive somewhere, you will probably continue to drive that same route in the future. But suppose the highway you follow becomes more and more clogged with traffic. If someone tells you about an alternate route that avoids the hassle of congested traffic and is altogether more pleasant, yet doesn't take longer than the first one, you're very likely to try out that new drive. If it turns out to be what you were told, then you're most likely to change your behavior and drive the new way from that point on. You have formed a new belief, that the new direction you follow to work is

92

better. Most important, you change because the new behavior fulfills your needs.

But the old routines, deeply embedded as automatic behavior, can be tenacious, underscoring the importance of making clear to people how a change fulfills their needs.

Years ago as a younger consultant I had an assignment working with a wonderful company that built hydroturbines. The company discovered that the grinding machines they had used for years would throw steel filings and other toxic debris and smoke back into the grinder's face. To improve working conditions and "do the right thing," management purchased rather expensive grinding machines with hoods that would reduce the health risk to the employees. To everyone's surprise the grinders didn't like the new hooded machines that were much safer and opted to continue using the old ones— even with all the health risk.

Logic would presuppose that the grinders would make a better more rational choice, but they didn't. Finally, with a new management policy and the support of the union, the grinders changed to the new machinery, but it took almost six months. Psycho-logic is very powerful and, even in an example such as this involving such a tangible change, we see how hard it is to gain alignment. With abstractions and mind-set changes, it is even more challenging because only the leader has the new purpose and values to provide direction.

The key to achieving these kinds of changes is not a management problem; it is an art form.

The Art of Causing Followership

The essence of instilling new beliefs, perception, and behavior in followers is "need-goal alignment." In this process, the leader works to align the satisfaction of the followers' needs with the goals for which the leader is responsible. Just as with an individual, if you can change organizational beliefs, then you can change the culture and subsequent behavior. By seeing clearly what the organization's goals are and the changes they call for, and by understanding your followers' needs, you gain the ability to link those needs to the goals by demonstrating how the new behavior will benefit the followers. If they see no benefit, they are unlikely to change their behavior, regardless of how inspiring a speaker you are.

The art of causing followership rests on three fundamental principles; they are simple, yet many leaders do not grasp them:

1. *People do what their minds and emotions tell them to do, not what the leader says to do.*
2. *The follower provides the motivation.*
3. *All motivation is self-serving.*

We'll look at these three principles in more details in the following sections.

Hypocrisy in Aligning Followers

One of the late Stephen Covey's maxims is to "first seek to understand before being understood." In other words, you must consider your followers' worldviews and needs if you want them to fully understand the new direction you are seeking and to motivate themselves with new behavior. Oversimplified and generalized, this wonderful statement can be not only misunderstood but too easily forgotten. As you come to understand the needs, beliefs, and desires of the people you need to influence, you create the opportunity to construct a well-thought-out leadership induction (a kind of communication) that will cause others to motivate themselves toward the goals for which you are responsible and, in many cases, accountable.

Preferring a habitual, "check-off-the-box" mentality, many companies and managers attempting to change direction, however, perceive the time and effort this understanding takes as inefficient. It is not. It is critical to achieving followership. You cannot successfully share vision and obtain changes in behavior without taking time to first understand. Yet time and again we see companies embark on a process of change to deal with new conditions only to neglect this important component.

Does the following scenario sound familiar?

A certain corporation regularly took inventory of where it stood relative to competitors in its market, and where it needed to go in light of economic cycles, market conditions, competitors' strategies, and the like. The company hired a well-regarded consulting firm to coordinate the process. The consultants spent many hours interviewing key managers, executives, and customers, and surveying the marketplace, conducting competent research. The result was a plan aimed at achieving competitive advantage, changing the firm's direction. The executive leadership conducted a few town-hall meetings, intended to encourage employees to buy in to the new company direction. Months after the final planning meetings, no significant change had taken place. Employees acted no differently from the way they had in the past. The executives had operated under the faulty assumption that "telling" others what needed to happen would lead them to change, ignoring the fact that what they said was always filtered through the old misaligned belief system, and the associated judgments and reactions.

Achieving the plan's goals relied on implementation by technically or administratively oriented managers who were trained in preparing budgets, compiling monthly reports, and setting quantitative goals. They had been hired to continue the success of the firm's founders and had never had much interest in learning about human behavior, regarding it as "touchy-feely stuff" they made time for only when they attended mandatory HR training events. They had received high-quality management training and were skilled in management techniques. But they had no idea how to implement the sound plan the consultants handed them. They had never worked to align human beliefs and behavior in a new direction with a clearly defined purpose and core values.

The result is predictable when neither executive leadership nor its managers grasp the need for changing minds. Declaring that leaders desire change and support new ways of doing things and then doing nothing to ensure those happen constitute a form of hypocrisy, and employees perceive it as such.

Ignoring Followers' Needs

The first principle of the art of causing followership points to a basic truth about human nature: what you as a leader say does not matter if you do not take into account what the minds and emotions of others tell them to do. Ignoring the psychological and emotional needs of followers is like running through an obstacle course blindfolded. The predominant leadership model in business and in many other organizations is built according to a control-authority design. In light of the psychological reality that people do only what they want to do, and what their past beliefs and mind tell them, this model produces employees who work only as hard as is necessary to avoid the consequences of disobedience. This is misalignment.

Behavior can be aligned, but the follower does it, not the leader. Until you get the mind and the heart (emotional) buy-in you will not get the courageous action you need and you will end up building a culture of hypocrisy. Shouting instructions louder, getting angry, or clarifying job descriptions is good for defining boundaries and division of labor, but not for changing behavior. Ignoring the psychological and emotional needs, it will only superficially change behavior.

A leader who neglects to take followers' psychological and social needs into account will be forced to spend a tremendous amount of energy merely to maintain the status quo. In that case, even though the leader may have a vision of the future for the organization and may have the courage to steer a different course, that leader will be stepping onto the path to that future alone. Recall the first point in the art of causing followership: you as a leader cannot achieve your goals alone; you must have the cooperation of others. If you visualize real leadership as jumping off the edge of the cliff to move beyond the quit zone, do you really want to jump by yourself?

Cross-Purposes

Beyond just not understanding what motivates followers, leaders can practice hypocrisy when they pursue courses that don't align with organizational values and purpose. A leader may not be clear on that purpose, espousing a belief or behavior that doesn't match the goals. On the other hand, sometimes leaders know what the purpose is and yet follow a different course, out of a personal agenda, or self-interest, or a reluctance to make clear the new behavior expected. In other words they throw the organization and others under the bus to be able to play the old game.

Remember, for example, the ego's defense mechanism of pleasing. A pleaser can fail to make clear to subordinates the new beliefs and behavior that the envisioned purpose entails, fearing that these will make the follower uncomfortable and possibly lead to an unfavorable perception of the leader. Certainly this type of leader will be reluctant to give negative performance feedback. Becoming self-aware means moving beyond the pleasing mentality to align beliefs and behavior with purpose, in the follower's own interest, as well as in the organization's.

This move can be difficult not only because of a desire not to displease followers but also because of the pleaser's own desires, which may conflict with the organization's greater purpose when the pleaser is the leader. Here's one example I have seen:

An entrepreneur we'll call Fred started a construction company, which in three short years reached 30 million dollars a year in revenues. Fred was a rising star in the industry, a great networker, salesman, and deal maker. Part of his company's initial success was due to his second in command, his operations manager, whom we'll call Terry, who didn't have the greatest people skills, but was naturally gifted at managing the business.

The company grew so fast that hiring competent people became a major issue. The company was forced to start hiring off the street just to fill positions, without taking time to find the right people for those positions. Terry became worried and told Fred he needed to slow down the sales so the company could keep up with customer service and other aspects of the overall business. Fred, however, was addicted to the thrill of the hunt in making sales and ignored Terry's warnings.

Leadership Beyond Belief

Eventually, Terry grew so frustrated over the increasing number of problems the rapid sales growth caused and Fred's refusal to listen to his advice that he quit. For a while, the company continued to grow mostly due to Fred's amazing ability to close deals. Finally, however, a number of projects began to come in behind schedule and with questionable quality. The manager Fred hired to replace Terry was a pleaser and did not deliver bad news to Fred. The company eventually developed financial problems as Fred continued to bring in business, but poor management left it unable to capture the profits. The company eventually had to downsize and then finally went out of business.

Fred's overly optimistic personality and "sunny-side up," denial-based defense mechanism worked well in sales, but it proved disastrous for leading the entire company. When Terry left, there was no source of honest performance feedback or timely decision making.

Fred was not aware enough to move beyond his need to be positive, in the context of the greater good of the company, or to appreciate and respond to Terry's honest feedback. He could not align his own behavior or his followers' with the organization's purpose.

Leaders also need to be aware of their peers' and subordinates' personalities; pleasers in those positions may try to satisfy a strong need to be appreciated, be seen as helpful and loyal, and be liked, and so they may be unable to express their concerns. As a result, they can become resentful captives of others' wishes and not contribute what might be their own valuable insights and self-generated energy to the organization's purpose. Instead, they contribute to a culture of hypocrisy. When they are at the top, it can get real bad, fast.

By the way, Fred learned his lesson and has again built a company. But this time he is enjoying great success and truly leads himself to look for blind spots and not run from them. In fact he told me a while back he spends a good bit of time uncomfortable in his executive meetings. He has developed the "stomach for success."

Integrity in Aligning Followers

To succeed in changing followers' behavior to align with the organization's goals, you need to present a pragmatic vision: a picture of future conditions that will positively affect the people you are asking to change. The picture must show, as well, the pitfalls of not changing soon enough. Followers also must clearly see the connection between the new behavior and processes and the bigger strategic picture—the purpose and goals. If they don't, then they may perceive your requests as arbitrary, particularly if the requests cause them pain. Your picture must present all these factors in images that are personally meaningful to your followers.

Causing change in human behavior is a simple proposition, really: the employees who are going to freely exert the most effort to change will be those who see that the perceived gain outweighs the perceived cost. In fact, we can phrase this as a formula, which Jim Farr and I shared in an article about followership and need-goal alignment (Farr and Grinnell 1994), which is handy to keep in the forefront of your mind when you're trying to lead people to change:

$$Human\ Effort\ to\ Change = Perceived\ Gain\ /\ Perceived\ Cost$$

If you're numerically inclined and can imagine calculating this formula in regard to a particular effort to change direction in an organization, and the human effort to change calculates out to be a decimal point and number, then the calculation tells you that the employee will not invest the effort. You want the answer to be a larger whole number, so to speak. The more gains you can demonstrate to employees—"what's in it for me" (their needs, mostly psychological and social)—the higher that number will be. To reduce the cost part of the equation as much as you can, you need to make sure that perceived costs have meaning in relation to the goals, have a clear purpose, and will be seen as resulting in a better future for the organization and for the employees in the long run. Many times this will require examples tied to the new values and the short-, medium-, and long-term positive effects of taking on this new behavior. Having a clear vision based on core values is important for this equation; it is essential for demonstrating benefits.

Harnessing the Power of Self-Motivation

Understanding the three principles of the art of causing followership is a prerequisite for being able to convey effectively the benefits this formula reveals to followers. To underscore the second principle, that followers provide the motivation, a simple but profound truth that leaders must grasp is this:

> *No leader can motivate others. A leader can only move followers to motivate themselves.*

Successful leaders are motivated to achieve goals. So are effective followers. An individual's efforts toward achieving a goal are done for personal, satisfying reasons. The ditch digger working past exhaustion and the other asleep holding the shovel under that shade tree are both equally motivated: one to work, one to sleep. At some level, all human action, even that of someone like Mother Teresa, fulfills a personal need and is self-serving.

This is not just wordplay. It is hugely significant in that leaders who believe they are the source of the motivation and the energy to achieve set themselves up for unnecessary frustration, energy loss, and decreased incentive for followers to motivate themselves and become more empowered. Who would you rather have be frustrated—the person you delegated responsibility to or you? If it's you, then you haven't done a good job empowering the follower. This is a psychological shift in perspective that is critically important, but that so few understand. Just look at how people become frustrated and how they talk. The most pernicious result of a leader's making him- or herself the source of the energy, motivation, and responsibility is that over time it weakens the followers' self-confidence and, consequently, they rely more and more on their boss. Of course, this supports many bosses' idealized self-image that they are powerful, smart, capable, instrumental, relevant, and so on. If a leader wants to effectively increase his or her span of control, he or she must master this key point: the follower provides his or her own motivation.

This insight implies the third principle, that *all motivation is self-serving*. Becoming aware of what drives the other people working with you is essential if you are to figure out how to align those followers' behavior with the envisioned goal, and then accomplish that alignment. Real leadership means creating a psychological environment that fosters the motivation of followers, which is why the number one qualification for being the successful leader of an organization is not understanding processes but understanding people.

We saw these principles in action in the 2012 Summer Olympics:

The U.S. men's basketball team faced great pressure to win another gold medal. The team included a group of NBA stars, though it also included some valuable role players who weren't big stars. Coach Mike Krzyzewski, longtime coach of the Duke University team, also author of a wonderful book on leadership called *The Gold Standard* (2009; see Jackson and Delehanty 1995 as well), has year in and year out coached players just out of high school. For the Olympic team, he was in charge of a group of millionaires in their twenties and thirties. Inspirational motivational techniques that work well with college players are not likely to work well with the pros—playing basketball in front of thousands is something they do every day for their job. "Coach K" clearly understood this point. The atmosphere he created on the team led the professional players to find their own motivation to win, and that motivation was apparent on television in the comments of some of the stars, who focused on playing for their country and being determined to win the medal. When asked by reporters how he motivated the NBA all-stars, Krzyzewski replied that he didn't have to do much—they motivated themselves. True enough, but the Olympic team has in the past had NBA stars who did not play well together as a team. Krzyzewski created the environment that led the players to motivate themselves. And clearly, the players appreciated the way he had gone about his task. Your professionals are no different.

Leadership Beyond Belief

Need-Goal Alignment

"Mapping the mental terrain" is a phrase we use to describe the process of understanding the follower's psychology, that is, his or her needs, mind-sets, beliefs, and values. With this "map" in hand, the real leader goes to work to align followers' needs with the organization's goals. This taps into each follower's own rich stores of motivation and commitment. A leader who can align goals with followers' needs will release the tremendous energy locked inside each human being. Every person contains potential energy of this sort and, if you can understand what drives that person and then align your actions accordingly, you will benefit from self-motivated behavior and commitment that will help move the organization toward that future you all believe in. Leadership that creates need-goal alignment opens the way for people to advance far beyond what they would produce to satisfy the demands of authority (figure 7).

You can take advantage of two aspects of human psychology in working to align followers with the organization's purpose: most people enjoy working with other people, and most people want to achieve goals. According to research by Sanvido and Konchar (1999), goals are both tangible and intangible. They relate to achieving successful financial, technical, professional, and human outcomes and building a positive brand in the minds of both customers and employees. When employees believe they are contributing to a positive outcome that fulfills their own needs, builds a successful company that provides meaningful employment to many people, and serves a socially beneficial purpose, they are more likely to motivate themselves to contribute to this effort. If you have a clear view of the organization's purpose, goals, and core values, you are more likely to be able to articulate that purpose and those goals in a way that relates to your followers' desire to work on a team and their drive to achieve goals.

To return to the formula on the effort to change, if you can align your followers' needs with the organization's goals, creating an environment in which followers will achieve those goals when they satisfy their own needs, the rewards will far outweigh the costs. Releasing the energy and motivation of your followers will build a team of aligned followers who are committed to doing whatever it takes to achieve the organization's purpose. As Mackey and Sisodia relate from their experience, "a business built on love and care rather than stress and fear, [where] team members are passionate and committed to their work" is one in which employees' "days race by in a blur of focused intensity, collaboration, and camaraderie. Far from becoming depleted and burned out, they find themselves at the end of each day newly inspired and freshly committed to . . . the opportunity to be part of something larger than themselves, to make a difference, to craft a purposeful life while earning a living" (2013:31).

Aligning the Organization

The real leader expands his or her self-awareness and awareness of what drives his or her followers. The task of alignment, however, is broader than those two aspects. The real leader needs to keep a strong, holistic sense of organizational needs and movement at the forefront of consciousness at all times. As with self-awareness and awareness of others, holistic alignment of the organization begins with self-examination on this broader scale. Examining your organization is similar to the way you reflect on your own beliefs and habitual behavior: *why* does it behave the way it does? What beliefs, formed in its early years to confront conditions at the time, continue to govern the behavior of executives, their subordinates, and their employees? Are the values, systems, and processes aligned?

Constructing flowcharts of business practices will give you a head start on recognizing patterns and identifying behavior that doesn't necessarily contribute to the future success of the company. Ask what purpose these habitual practices serve. Will they serve us when we are twice the size we are now? Dig deeper, too, to try to understand what led the founders to implement certain ways of doing things that became corporate policies and culture. What problems were they trying to solve? Are those problems still relevant? Why did their customers choose to support them instead of others for many years of success? At the deepest level, such an examination seeks to answer this question: what is the company's purpose? What are its values? *Why*, in other words, does it exist? What need in society does

103

it seek to fulfill? Does the company have a different purpose now from its original one? Are our values being lived or espoused now? The answers to these foundational questions give you the starting point for alignment of systems, processes, and people.

Start with Purpose to Be "On-Purpose"

Stephen Covey's most famous axiom is to "start with the end in mind." I put it this way:

> You can't really start the organizational change pro-
> cess until you get the new idea (and expectations) into
> the mind of your management team, and then the new
> expectations for behavior into the minds of their em-
> ployees with the essential caveat that we will learn as
> we go, and as Robert Quinn says: "build the bridge as
> we walk on it."

Success in this task, as we saw in the example earlier, requires different skills from the technical and administrative abilities managers typically bring to their jobs. If they want to succeed, leaders need to understand that the skill of aligning the motivation of employees with the new direction and goals of the organization requires above all subtle perception; the more perceptive of human behavior a leader becomes, the easier achieving such alignment becomes. It also requires solid knowledge of human nature and good values. Without a proper understanding of what it takes to lead people to want to change, then failure is the most likely outcome. This usually happens when leaders focus on the more familiar and tangible process of changing systems and processes instead of changing minds, using the processes as an anvil against which to change minds.

Creating the environment in which subordinates and their employees will motivate themselves is a crucial step in alignment toward the goals. When followers see the vision clearly, understand what being on-purpose looks like, and believe the changes it brings will benefit them, the leader's job is much easier. But it's not done. The leader must keep people's focus on the vision and keep followers' efforts aligned with the goals. As leaders and followers move forward, how they communicate will determine how successful they are.

Hypocrisy in Aligning the Organization

Thus far, one implication of alignment should be clear: a leader can be aware regarding both self and organization; have a clear sense of the organization's purpose now and of the new beliefs, values, and behavior necessary to accomplish the related goals; and have a good understanding of what motivates his or her followers; but if that leader doesn't convey the purpose, beliefs, behavior, and benefits effectively to followers, the organization is not likely to thrive in the long run. Clear communication is as necessary a component of alignment as awareness, both to begin the process of change and to sustain it. As with awareness, though, executive leadership and managers often are not willing to take time to think about how to communicate effectively and then expend the energy to do so.

Failing to make clear to followers the organization's purpose and, as best you can, what it requires in values, new beliefs, and behavior is a prescription for a failure to tap the self-generated energy necessary to achieve the goals associated with that purpose.

Focusing for Change

When leadership doesn't take the time to make sure managers are fully aligned with each other regarding how to carry out change and that they then align followers with the organization's purpose and future beliefs, strategic planning, as we saw in the earlier example, isn't likely to be implemented well. If the management team isn't clear on the "playbook" for change and if employees do not know what is expected of them, neither group is likely to align to execute change well—if at all. In many cases, though, managers are too busy with their managerial duties and so don't take adequate time for effective communication, treating peers and employees as if they were soothsayers able to read tea leaves.

Executives who aren't clear themselves on how to proceed will shoot from the hip, so to speak, dropping work randomly on subordinates, failing to follow agreed-on strategic and tactical plans, and failing to follow new policy. When they do, employees lose discipline and focus, not knowing what the priorities are or how to change their behavior.

One possible result is the unnecessary creation of anxiety. Executives have usually been involved in the planning from the beginning of the process and this involvement usually reduces their anxiety by the time the plan is announced. Therefore, they can easily fail to empathize with the angst felt by employees on lower levels, forgetting the anxiety they themselves felt in the beginning. Amid the uncertainty of change, especially when accurate information is scarce, people tend to exaggerate the scope and implications of the change to match the discomfort they experience.

Another result of a failure to communicate effectively and truthfully is employee resistance. Not only does this undercut the effort to align and waste a great deal of time and energy, it is unnecessary, because it could have been easily avoided in the first place with effective communication.

Real leaders should understand, too, that communication and trust among peers is just as important as trust between leaders and followers. Horizontal flow of information needs to match vertical flow, upward and downward. Here is where we often fall again within the shadow of corpocentrism.

Crossing Boundaries

Just as ego strength can provide necessary drive in individuals, corpocentrism can be a positive force creating unity, alignment, and teamwork in an organization. But when the activities it generates equate to ego defense mechanisms, it creates boundaries and political maneuvering between organizational units. When these boundaries are in place, they result in the organizational silos that restrict the free flow of information between units. That flow is critical for the perceptual and behavioral agility that enables coordination of effort and efficient use of resources.

When the organization experiences hypocrisy instead of integrity, individuals view information as conferring power, and they hoard it or manipulate it out of self-interest. Followers feel a fear of retribution and hide failures rather than learn from them. Because of a lack of accurate information, people don't know how to decide on courses of action, and decisions they do make are aimed at maintaining their comfort zones through politics.

Look at repeated mistakes with customers, technical errors, lack of discipline in administrative systems, problems in planning, and difficulties in coordination and execution, and you will very likely find troublesome vertical or horizontal relationships. There are many significant mental, emotional, and political barriers that keep people from hearing each other. Overcoming those barriers is difficult if you don't believe in the touchy feely stuff—if you don't understand the logic of human emotion and behavior and instead think business is mostly rational. In fact, it isn't; it's mostly psychological.

Political Resistance

Another aspect of organizational alignment and hypocrisy that leaders need to be aware of is the extent to which politics enters change initiatives when many within the organization don't understand what the process entails and what it's intended to achieve, or even when they do, but fail to act with integrity. Organizational integrity can be thought of as the hull of a ship. When a unit or person is out of alignment, it is as if a huge steel plate is loosened and water rushes in. The ship slows and eventually, if the plate is not repaired, it can sink. Acting with integrity can be a very difficult task, as there are political consequences for changing.

A few years ago I worked with a well-known and excellent leader who was brought into an established culture to help turn it around, as it was headed into a financial nightmare (not of his making). As he pushed forward in the right ways and provided the logic behind the cost cutting, as well as the need for revenue enhancement, he met resistance. Several of the more politically entrenched senior people started rumors, completely unfounded, about his incompetence. Many in the division, even though they knew his path was the right one, would not stand up and state that publicly—even though, without the realization of his efforts, they were headed for a financial nightmare. They knew that if he was fired and they had agreed with the changes he suggested, the political power brokers in their organization would remember and limit their careers. Integrity—the word is easy to say, but the act is very difficult when people are defending past approaches and beliefs full of fear and excellent rationalizations for their behavior.

Integrity in Aligning the Organization

Alignment of the organization begins with listening and communication that is both effective, truthful, and nondefensive. If an accurate flow of information from below helps leaders become aware and gain perspective through listening, an accurate flow in the reverse direction is necessary for leaders to present the picture of the new purpose, show followers how the changes it requires benefit them, and indicate the new behavior that the change will require and how everyone will carry out that behavior. To achieve these ends, the leader needs to illuminate the path ahead in a plan that everyone clearly understands.

Because markets, organizations, and people are dynamic, not static, alignment is an ongoing process that may require further changes in beliefs and behavior as conditions change. Thus, you need to constantly work to be aware of what is happening around you *now*, adjust the plan if necessary, and make sure everyone understands the adjustments. As the adage goes, "plan the work and work the plan." But I add this: in light of purpose and values, adjust it when you learn you need to.

To inspire confidence, planning must reflect awareness. That is, the plan must demonstrate a full understanding of the risks associated with the positive changes you're aiming to achieve. It must relate to them truthfully, and must include sound strategies to manage the risk as much as possible. Many executives miss the importance of this step, but followers will not follow unless leaders can maintain their trust and confidence in an atmosphere of uncertainty and change; many managers don't fully grasp how vital communication is in this effort, and even fewer grasp the essence of communication.

Filtering and Framing

Listening and communication needs to be leaders' greatest time investment during change; if it is, it will certainly provide a huge return on that investment. Companies that take the time, and spend the money, to "overcommunicate" through newsletters, announcements, and special events, for example, help expedite change—but *this effort is not enough.* Management should seek a deeper level of employee commitment and energy. This is done through open-minded and sincere listening. Slogans and written material, though necessary, on their own will not enable the organization to succeed in reaching its new goals.

Senior managers often get frustrated when this proves true, even though they have often tried to communicate. What they fail to understand is a crucial truth:

Communication is not what you tell followers; it is what they hear (through their mind-sets and beliefs).

If you as a leader are aware, then you will understand that what you say is not received as pure information; people always filter what they hear through self-interest. Do they perceive the information you convey as likely to help them or hurt them in their professions and in their lives? Understanding how people motivate themselves is essential to knowing how you should communicate with them and what they will hear.

In communicating why the change is necessary and what the purpose and goals are, always keep in mind need-goal alignment and the formula for generating human effort to change. You must properly position change in the minds of your followers; how management frames and sequences change can comfort employees and make the distasteful tasteful, or at least make it palatable. Proper positioning entails understanding what motivates followers and making the benefits of change clear. But it also means being truthful about the changes ahead; alignment will not happen without trust among leaders, their peers, and their followers.

Trust and Relationships

Being truthful and keeping agreements not only creates trust, it also reduces anxiety about change, since fear of the unknown leads employees to exaggerate the changes required. Knowing what change lies ahead often reassures followers that it will not be as drastic as they feared. If they have an accurate picture of the path ahead, they're more likely to convince themselves they can follow it.

The connection between trust and communication is reciprocal, creating a self-sustaining process. Honest dialogue is necessary for trust between people to grow, and listening is its basis; and trust is necessary for ongoing communication. Without honest dialogue, deeper than what most organizations experience, you will not find greater alignment for your shared purpose.

Trust and communication are central to countering the force of corpocentrism. Establishing the environment in which they will flourish requires effective leadership development of the kind this book outlines, to create awareness and foster growth of strong personal relationships that produce mutual trust. Regardless of how strong corpocentrism is in an organization, the key to breaking down the barriers to open and honest communication across units is building personal relationships through strong leadership.

The Three Levels of Alignment

Alignment happens on three levels—mind, behavior, and emotions—and it must take place on all three levels for leaders, subordinates, and followers in order to succeed. This full alignment is of primary importance for leaders.

Alignment in the mind springs from becoming aware. When you are aware, you can identify the corporate values and your personal beliefs, and you can choose right ones that align with organizational purpose and need and that are based on the highest good. These are beliefs that, when you follow them, will drive your realization of your purpose toward the chosen personal and organizational experience you and others want. It defines a way of living life toward success and a life experience you will be happy having lived. After choosing the right beliefs, you plan, decide, and work-behave toward a better future state more consciously. Thereby, you see more clearly on-purpose and off-purpose decisions, thus increasing the likelihood of success in gaining the experience you want as a person, the role you aspire to as a leader, and the future you envision for your organization.

Aligning also means changing your behavior to match the future beliefs and values you have identified. In the first place, changed behavior has to correspond to new belief if the envisioned purpose is to be accomplished. In the second place, as pointed out numerous times, followers are not likely to change their behavior, no matter how compelling the vision presented, if they see leaders failing to change their own behavior. The corollary to communicating the vision effectively is acting out the changes necessary to attain it. The behavior of leaders communicates as effectively as clear oral and written presentation.

Alignment in the emotions occurs when you come to genuinely "believe in the new belief" you are following, and your actions and relationships demonstrate that genuineness. Since hypocrisy can be unconscious and unintentional, this is the reason feedback and transparency is so important in helping people identify their blind spots and an organization or team spot the "unknown unknowns." When a leader enunciates a belief, shares a vision, announces a plan to achieve it, then doesn't carry through on the plan, the leader is not exhibiting integrity. Often the leader may even change behavior to some extent to appear in alignment, but the change is superficial, not really *felt* to the core. The leader may fully intend to change and follow up, but doesn't.

Only when a leader is driven by this new belief, compelled to change and act consistently out of conscious purpose reinforced by conviction, does alignment occur fully and convincingly. Only then will others emulate the belief and behavior, and jump with the leader out of the quit zone. Until that point, their full trust and followership do not exist.

This emotional sense of belief displays integrity in the alignment of belief and behavior. As mentioned earlier, on the hull of a wooden ship, if one of the planks is loose, the whole ship is in jeopardy. This is the basic level of the word *integrity* and its purpose. All three levels of alignment demand integrity in specific senses like this. Alignment also requires integrity in its more general sense, what employees and the public expect. Espousing alignment but not behaving differently or not having heartfelt alignment will jeopardize the potential impact of the strategy. Saying one thing but doing or feeling another leaks potential out of the organization.

Most leaders want to be seen as honest and truthful, particularly if they want to remain in business for any length of time. To build a foundation of trust, real leaders align their decisions and their actions with the good of their employees and the greater good of the organizations, customers, and communities they serve. They do the right thing even when no one is looking, when the chance of getting caught is minimal, and when right action is unenforceable. You are vulnerable in business when the performance of a partner, employee, or supplier is not perceived as trustworthy; real leaders understand that truth and how that perception interferes with alignment with the envisioned purpose. Once the reputation of being untrustworthy is out in the public domain, it is only a matter of time until the brand ceases to carry weight and the business begins to fail.

If, on the other hand, trust permeates your organization, it is on the way to fulfilling its purpose, and serving its members and the society beyond. And in that journey, you and your followers can find success and satisfaction.

Seek Alignment

If you believe your unit or team or organization is weak in seeking alignment, here are some recommendations.

1. Have the team read the "One-Team" section, "Mutual Accountability," in chapter 3 of this book. Hold a discussion. Make sure the members of your team understand that to help or hurt a teammate is to help and hurt the enterprise and eventually themselves. Work this over and over with them until they understand this point.

Seek Alignment

2. Once your strategy and mission are clear, have a third party come in and help you with a "climate" type of inside-out planning session to develop a focus for changes to systems, processes, and behavior to align with the new direction. This is a great team-building opportunity for your leadership team, but more importantly, if the interviews and subsequent actions are done right, it helps align the people who report up to the leadership team.

3. When someone on the team talks openly and honestly about his or her misalignment, thank the person, then work to find common ground.

4. When meetings get emotionally stuck by someone on the team who is "off-purpose" or who disrupts team dynamics, immediately begin coaching that person back into alignment—or off the team. Your job is to ensure that you have the best team, one on which all the members support each other.

5. Talk about the three levels of alignment: conceptual, behavioral, and emotional.

6. When you do training of any sort within the organization, make sure it is tied to your business or strategic plan. Empower those who report to you to lead the sessions.

7. Refer to your team-building events as "alignment sessions."

8. Read *Five Dysfunctions of a Team* by Patrick Lencioni (2002). Hold discussions regularly about the concept as it relates to your team. Make sure to focus on "trust" and "forgiveness," as these are the basis of true teamwork.

9. Have cross-functional units read the "Big 10 Collaborative Behaviors" in appendix 4.

Chapter 5

Expanding Awareness of Self and Others—the Basis of Leadership

> *Genuine self-awareness involves a free consciousness that is open-minded and calm in the face of uncertainty, . . . that can see current patterns of habitual behavior and the outcomes, good and bad, they create.*

Many people think they are aware when they are not. They mistake personality awareness or cultural awareness for self-awareness. But read self-awareness involves far more: it requires a free consciousness that is open-minded and calm amid uncertainty, able to observe clearly and maintain perspective, resisting the urge to default to habit or uninformed judgment. It is able to step past the ego's defenses and recognize the sources of decision and behavior. By contrast, being without self-awareness leads us to behave as myopic automatons who react instead of lead, thereby falling into the trap of avoidable errors and unintended consequences that no one wants.

What we are unaware of in ourselves controls us and our decisions and resulting actions. As we become more aware of our patterns of habitual behavior driven by belief, our personality as well as our mechanisms of ego defense, we create a "crack" that we can peek through to feel new opportunity and the potential, once we realize it requisite to achieve our purpose. Knowledge and experience are great teachers, but if they are not backed by awareness of the fundamental nature of the mind, then we are still at the mercy of the deeper system that quickly forms habit, thereby reducing awareness. As mentioned before, this is why history repeats itself. The content and circumstances may change, but it is just memory revisited by unaware leaders generation after generation. Many try to break the cycle with good intention, only to fail again because of a lack of fundamental self-awareness of the beliefs that drive their perceptions, decisions—in other words, them.

But when we know our minds, our beliefs, and the mind's habitual bias, as well as behavioral strengths and weaknesses and how these manifest in behavior, we then have the chance to make different choices, avoid negative unintended consequences, and realize our intended outcomes with much greater probability of longer-term success.

Reading People

Knowing yourself will make you a better leader, but you must know the minds of others as well to become truly effective. For that reason, this book is not a simple manual on how to create conditions whereby people choose to motivate themselves to align with goals of the leader. Certainly this is an important aspect of leadership, and the book discusses it, in the context of the Grinnell Leadership Vitality Model. But it is not the essence. The foundation of leading other people to attain your organization's goals is awareness. As pointed out in an article written by Jim Farr and me, "The Art of Causing Followership" (1994), the dictum about self-awareness applies equally to knowing other people's minds in order to understand what drives their behavior, perceptions, and actions. Real leadership requires the leader to align the work of others with his or her goal by understanding what actions on the leader's part will elicit the necessary motivation to achieve it. And to do so, the leader must gain an awareness of how individuals' minds work and the ways their perceptions and behavior cause them to interact with and relate to each other.

Ultimately, if you are to be a real leader, you must focus not only on reaching your own potential but also on enabling the members of the team around you to reach their own potential. True leadership is the art of causing followership. A potential leader asks, "How do I get individuals to do what I need them to do?" A real leader asks, "What can I say or do to get individuals to cause them to motivate themselves to do what I need them to do?"

A real leader must build what I call the One-Team (2012). Members of the One-Team grasp how we are all connected, particularly on a local, organizational level. They are acutely aware of their vulnerability to their teammates' performance and of their teammates' vulnerability to their performance. They understand that because we are connected, whether a team works smoothly together as a One-Team determines whether the organization attains its goal—indeed, perhaps even whether the organization survives.

They abdicated their leadership responsibility for political or psychological reasons.

When you reach that deeper place from where you see yourself clearly and understand how other minds work, then you will grasp two truths: first, leadership requires integrity. The perennial knowledge that has come down to you in the form of moral precepts to act with integrity is true. Those involved in the Enron scandal and the mortgage crisis behaved in habitual, seemingly safe ways, likely without self-awareness. In doing so, they abdicated leadership for one reason or another that they were unaware of, or unable to perform for political or psychological reasons. (In fact, someone who knew Ken Lay told me his problem was he was unaware of what was going on under him at Enron. The key point is that he was unaware.) But they also neglected lessons they'd learned from parents, teachers, and others as they grew up. One of the primary questions of leadership is this: how can people, on both small and large scales, do the right thing better? Second, practicing real leadership leads to a more

116

satisfying life. That happy leaders are good leaders is no accident. When you lead from that deep place of calm awareness and clear chosen values, you create conditions for better lives for yourself, the other members of your team, the organization as a whole, and the greater society in which we are all connected. We can turn the earlier phrase around: a good leader is a happy leader.

Although this book concentrates on leadership of an organization, acting with integrity and creating conditions for a better tomorrow have ramifications beyond the organization's success. No matter whether a company is large or small, it operates today in a global context, including a global economy. We are all connected. For a company to flourish, it must adapt to changing conditions. Just like a species, an organization cannot survive unless it makes smart adaptations. Leadership encapsulates the adaptive force of an organization; it sets direction and changes course so that the organization can survive, and it reshapes behavior so that the organization can succeed. Those organizations that can't adapt fast enough will eventually die (Quinn 1996). The critical quality for adapting is agility; and reaching the deeper place of self-awareness is a critical step in enabling a leader to respond to challenges with agility (Grinnell 2010).

The Old Ways Won't Work in a New World

The disastrous consequences of the failure of leadership in recent years leave no doubt that actions based on instinct, greed, and habitual patterns of behavior for the purpose of "survival" will instead lead in the opposite direction. The consequences of this behavior are now too devastating for us to continue to think and act in the old reflexive way. Just as it does on personal and organizational levels, awareness applies on this broader global level. What we do affects someone in Japan. What someone in Japan does affects us. Decisions made in isolation with limited information from an egocentric, "corpocentric," or ethnocentric basis will lead to *our* eventual failure. We can't afford to merely "learn about" other cultures. We must go deeper, to understand what beliefs and culture in themselves are and how to effectively work within and beyond them.

And as noted earlier, these requirements apply not just on a grand scale, within large corporations where the behavior of leaders affects thousands. They apply in the store with a few employees. They apply in the start-up with five or six employees and a promising product and strategy. They apply in a department of a small company or a hospital or a bank where ordinary people struggle with how to behave in their jobs every day, in ways that affect other people, in their own organization and outside it, in the shape of customers and suppliers.

As we move into an increasingly complex, greatly challenging, and uncertain future, we are in dire need of leaders who understand that they serve the requirements of an interdependent social system, not just their own reputations and identities (egos), their organizations, or their ethnic groups, other kinds of constituencies, or countries. We need leaders who are aware—of themselves and human nature; who focus on purpose and values—their own and their organizations'; and who strive for alignment and accountability. To develop them, we need a new leadership paradigm that transcends self-interest and cultural bias, and we need it to emerge rapidly. This is the fundamental leadership challenge of the twenty-first century. And what I address in this book.

A few years ago, Amita Poole, former chief of staff of the Architect of the Capitol, pointed out in a private conversation that the way we run our organizations, large and small, has a direct impact on the fabric of our society, in both the short term and the long. Poole told me that when leaders act well, "however small the right action is, it strengthens the fabric of society." This observation extends to the global society. The way we run our businesses as well as our families helps weave or tear apart the fabric that underlies people's happiness, liberty, prosperity, and self-determination. This book focuses on leading business organizations and provides a perspective and set of practices that affect the daily interactions of leaders and followers. But because of the way we are all connected now, the leadership principles it presents have an impact on our global society. Effective human leadership of people and organizations applies on that larger

118

stage as well. The Angel Model (see chapter 1, and also chapter 6) will help you cut through all the crap about how to lead and understand what leadership really is and how you can apply its lessons to create the better future we all want.

Chapter 6
Jump-Start Real Leadership
The Challenge of Real Leadership

Corporations spend millions of dollars every year on consultants and marketing firms to help them find the right competitive angle by pinpointing competitors' weaknesses and focusing corporate strengths in those areas. They "do the numbers" and find acquisitions to support their strategy or they grow organically. Further, companies can try to find technical advantage brought on by new technology. What these approaches really focus on is marketing and management techniques and what we call directional or technical/scientific leadership, which is essential, but which is not real leadership, which I highlight in this book.

Real leadership is the adaptive force within an organization, the process for successful change of human perspective, thinking, and behavior.

Real leadership is not the same as competent management, or even directional leadership—though organizations need these functions done well too. Real leadership is something beyond these; it is, in effect, the adaptive force within an organization, creating the process that can change human perspective, thinking, and behavior. Rather than simply seeking a skilled analysis of competitive angles, it requires a commitment to act without the security of accepted behavior, to step beyond the usual boundaries in order to align the organization with its envisioned purpose and values. And more importantly than comprehending concrete factors of, say, balance sheets, profit and loss, or supply and demand pricing, making this commitment is always personal, even when other people are involved. Few do it well, and they usually wait until crisis forces change at the higher cost of unnecessary and unintended waste of human time, energy, and resources.

Not all organizational leadership is real leadership. Some form of leadership, after all, is inevitable: someone has to make decisions. But a "decision" can occur by default, a failure to act, what I call "indecision making," and the resulting non-action constitutes a decision. We see this indecision making happen all the time, when leaders of organizations abide by conventional patterns of behavior within the organization because doing so seems the safe course. However, when an organization has to adapt to changing conditions, it's not so safe after all.

Real leadership recognizes that changing or transforming an organization requires a change in mind, a change in belief, and a change in behavior. Such change is usually rife with uncertainty. Here's an example, from a company we worked with, of what can happen to struggling companies when leaders make the necessary commitment to venture outside the safe harbor of accepted behavior:

> The company had grown rapidly for years through acquisitions of both domestic and international companies, but these acquisitions hadn't worked well. Eventually this dynamic resulted in numerous changes in the "C suite," as well as frequent downsizing to stay afloat. Most of the remaining employees (over twenty thousand) had become cynical and disenchanted, and if the market hadn't been weak, many would have left if they could have. Even though the company was large, and had a cadre of competent professionals, it was relatively unknown and unrecognized as a key player in the markets it served.

Leadership Beyond Belief

At this point, it appointed a new CEO. When she took the position, she committed personally to "real leadership." She saw that the organization must change and adapt if it was to thrive in its fast-changing field. It took five years, however, for a majority of her executive team to fully understand what "real leadership" meant. These were not slow learners. They had gone to the best schools and considered themselves leaders. They had repeated trendy terms, such as "accountability," "feedback," "transparency," and "collaboration" for years. They understood these terms conceptually. What they had not done in their careers, though, was take the personal and perceived and possibly actual political risk of acting in a truly different way in the face of uncertain support. Sure, their performance and that of their company had improved over the past five years, but it had taken this long for most of them to intuitively grasp that real leadership requires a fundamental personal shift in perspective and behavior.

Suddenly, when the majority became aware, and understood this requirement at a deep level, the company underwent a quantum leap. Changing mind and behavior in a new direction transformed the individual executives, then the organization. The dynamics within the executive team were different. The level of truth telling was much higher; as they didn't compulsively seek advocacy for their decisions and actions, they stopped compromising and became accountable. Analytics now mixed with emotion. Energy had increased. The executives broke the spell of past approaches and cut away the safety net of habitual expectations, both personal and cultural.

As a result, irrational politics diminished markedly, as these leaders no longer worried about being wrong, wasted energy defending their egos, or clung to past approaches. In the face of new challenges, the leaders displayed excitement instead of apathy. They could think both globally about the enterprise and about their own areas of responsibility and find right solutions. They were committed to the actions they proposed, and they followed through. And the company adapted successfully.

What happened in this corporation was not just change. It was transformation. Change is mowing the grass. Transformation is replacing the lawn. And the key to transformation is awareness. Without being aware of my personality or the lived corporate culture and its undergirding of beliefs, I can't see new options to support my organization's purpose more effectively (not to mention my own), and I don't know how to transform my behavior to align it with that purpose. Without being self-aware, I'm not aware of others. And if I'm unaware of others, I can't help them transform their behavior in alignment with our common purpose.

The Quit Zone

When leaders disrupt the deep sleep of habitual belief and behavior with conflicting intent, different information, and new behavior, they often meet the quite normal resistance of established habits and beliefs, first within themselves and then from others. Without a deep understanding of self and human nature, corporate leaders continue developing a plan that, although it may be clear, ignores the human element, which is akin to walking blindfolded in a minefield. As a result, at the critical moment, the company fails to change course in the direction the leaders—and often everyone else—see as obvious. In many cases, those leaders end up unnecessarily losing money, market share, even their business and their personal health. Jim Farr called this hesitation "leadership lag." (I discussed this concept more fully in chapter 3.) It inevitably leads to what Robert Quinn in *Deep Change* calls a "slow death" for businesses, a death brought on by clinging to behavior we are accustomed to yet that isn't leading us to an experience we want. I call this area where the new path is glimpsed, but avoided, the "quit zone." Figure 7 depicts this entire process. Most of us operate in a memory-based zone, which is comfortable—it's based on beliefs we've accrued in the past. The quit zone, though, is a place of uncertainty and therefore for many a cause of anxiety, but it is also

Figure 7. The Real Leader's Jump and the Quit Zone

a place of exhilaration when we glimpse the future that could exist.

It is a potential base for launching us onto the leader path—if we have the courage to follow that path. The quit zone is an area full of creative tension (see Senge 1990): the future is unknown, but if we are aware of ourselves, our core values, other people, and the purpose of our organization, we can form a new belief, one that aligns with our purpose, and engage in new behavior. It helps to visualize the quit zone as ending in a cliff that overlooks the leader path. What separates a real leader—for example, in business, a successful entrepreneur—is the ability to jump off the edge of the cliff in the quit zone and start a new venture or expand an existing one when success is uncertain and when chosen values, behavior, and beliefs are unproven. If it were easy, others would have done it already.

Unsurprisingly, many leaders become uneasy at the idea of leaving the certainty of past approaches and entering the quit zone and the real leader's path. In "jumping" from the past onto the leader path beyond through the quit zone, the leader must "intentionally"

124

embrace untested behaviors and unproven beliefs. But to avoid this embrace is to fail to provide real leadership; it is akin to "changing the deck chairs on the *Titanic* and expecting to avoid calamity." This is why there are very few real leaders, although there are many managers who call themselves leaders.

Identifying what real leadership requires is the critical first step in enabling more people to know how to become real leaders. Understanding what real leadership consists of provides a target that helps people focus on what they need to do to become real leaders. But don't underestimate the challenges: making the jump is difficult; sticking to the old beliefs is too easy, and excuses and rationalizations, such as the following, are readily at hand:

- "Things are going well now, so let's not have a third party do an anonymous climate study and planning event. Let's spend our time and money elsewhere."
- "What the hell, speaking up, even though I really disagree, may piss them off and would make me uncomfortable, so I'll just say nothing and keep my blood pressure down."
- "You know, that's not a really big violation of our agreed behaviors; I'll let it slip this time."
- "If I tell him his organization is out of alignment with our strategy, he might not advocate for me in the future and may even undermine me. I'll just compromise."
- "We need to do more research to make sure we have certainty of outcome before we launch."
- "I don't have enough power to get that to happen."
- "We have a new management team, and we are in recession, and I don't want to rock the boat and be seen as a troublemaker."

The force of this inertia, this indecision making, is why, once you become aware of how your mind works and what drives your behavior, aligning your behavior with the purpose glimpsed in the future where the leader path (unknown but believed in) will take you becomes the inescapable task if you want to succeed.

125

Leadership Beyond Belief

Aligning your own behavior, however, is not enough. You also must align the behavior of those working with you. Successfully aligning the behavior of others requires you to practice the art of causing followership. (See chapter 4 for a discussion of this art.)

To equip yourself to align behavior with purpose, you have to fulfill two conditions. First, you have to see a goal the organization must drive toward in order not only to survive but also to thrive. In other words, you must hold an "intention" or belief keyed to the future—a view of where the leader path will take you and the organization. You must have the felt desire for a different experience than you are having or see coming. And then you need, as best you can, to perceive what specific actions should occur to accomplish that change. A stumbling point here is that many people expect to have a clear step-by-step plan that will not change before they take the jump. This is not possible and people need to understand what Robert Quinn points out, that there must be agreement to "building the bridge as we walk on it." In other words, expect feelings of uncertainty and potential changes in plans, but don't wait for perfection or complete clarity before jumping. That is, learn and adapt as you go, but commit to the better future together.

Promise persistence, not perfection.

Those millions of dollars that companies spend on consultants to figure out the right angle can lead to excellent plans toward a better future. When these plans fail, they fail most often because managers can't execute the plans, and the primary reason they can't is the failure of people to act in new ways that align with the better idea. Often these managers will promise certainty when instead they should promise persistence, learning as we go, and doing the right things. When followers come to believe that you are a realist, are truthful, and understand their concerns, needs, interests, and ideas, then they come to trust you more fully and become more willing to try new behavior. Coupled with this, if you can show those who work with you that the new behavior you are asking for helps them—not only the goals of the organization but also their own mid- and longer-term interests and needs—then you have taken a step to help the

126

organization reach the desired future state. (See chapter 4 for more discussion of the concepts involved in causing followership.)

Becoming aware of why you and others act as you do, forming a vision of where the organization can go and developing new beliefs from that vision, clarifying core values and engaging in new behavior aligned with those new beliefs and values—these constitute the tools you need to help you lead yourself and others through the quit zone on the leader path. To give you and your organization the final push to make that jump successfully, you need one final tool. You, your colleagues, your followers, everyone in the organization needs to be accountable. "Accountability," I noted earlier, is a trendy word; but for real leadership, it has a specific meaning. It doesn't mean simply that your followers will be judged for their work. Limiting the meaning of "accountability" to that idea is likely to be counterproductive. Followers who work only as hard as necessary to avoid punishing consequences—and who are motivated by no other force from within—are unlikely to achieve great results. The concept must have broader scope. In the first place, you are accountable as a leader to yourself for making sure you keep the goal clearly in mind and keep your actions aligned with that goal. Accordingly, the other members of your leadership team are accountable to themselves foremost, to make sure they stay aligned with the goal, and they are accountable to their peers as members of a team.

The Grinnell Organizational Vitality Model

As noted in chapter 1, I call the model illustrating the concepts I've presented the Grinnell Organizational Vitality Model. Others call it the "Angel Model" because people have commented to me that it resembles an angel in shape, which seemed to me a nice touch, since it's a model of something that will help people in their lives, a "guardian angel" of sorts. In this model, expanded awareness forms the foundation of every other part of real leadership, and all the stages build toward fulfilling the purpose, the pinnacle toward which the pyramid is constructed. Alignment builds on that foundation of awareness, while at the same time being guided by the top of the pyramid, the purpose. In this model, the jump constitutes an area between alignment and accountability. In other words, aligning behavior with new belief requires ongoing accountability if we are to jump successfully. All three "A" levels are necessary to build the model, and it's not complete without the top. Without awareness, I am blind to that which drives me and the organization. I have interpersonal blind spots and I am blind to options or the need to change to create a different outcome. And I certainly can't take advantage of other options because I don't know how to transform my behavior to align my own and others' with the organization's purpose. In short, if I don't see or know it I can't address it as a leader.

Once I am self-aware and aware of others, however, I will realize how to align my behavior and cause others to align theirs with the mission. Without knowing how to align behavior, mine and others', I can't be accountable and neither can anyone else working with me because we don't know what to be accountable to. When I do know how to align behavior, then I need to be accountable to our purpose, myself, and my associates; they need to be accountable to me, to themselves, and to their colleagues too.

Being aware forms the base of the pyramid; it is the foundation that leadership builds on, including purpose: you can't put a top on a pyramid if there's no foundation. The reason the pinnacle of the pyramid is being on-purpose is that without this target, people have no way of judging their behavior except against the past: memory and habitual responses and beliefs. That is why you often hear real leaders asking frequently of themselves and others, "Are we 'on-purpose' with this decision and taking right action in alignment with purpose?"

Figure 2 in chapter 1 presents the stages of leadership in pyramid form—each stage builds on the previous one, to show the logical connection from awareness through service to customers, partners in success, and the social environment. Although the model is simple, the actual picture is more complex. These stages interpenetrate; just like alignment, on-purpose leadership flows out of awareness. You must be aware in order to improve your clarity about the purpose—yours, your followers', and the organization's. And just as you can't change to more fully align behavior until you are aware, you can't align it until you have a firm sense of what the purpose is. The purpose, which includes your chosen core values, also fills out the framework of accountability: you and everyone else are not accountable for your behavior in the abstract, as in whether you're following a time clock.

You're accountable for whether your behavior matches the purpose and is likely to advance the change achieving it requires. The more people are truly aware and aligned with the purpose, the greater the probability that the real leader's intention will be realized. Indeed, people in the organization are increasingly likely to feel certain that it will. And since you're heading into an unknown future, with success uncertain, which typically generates tension and fear, if you can create and maintain that feeling, and take advantage of creative tension and reduce the fear, the organization will be much likelier to accomplish its envisioned transformation.

Real leaders are the first willing to step out with untested behavior and unproven belief.

Remember that leadership is the adaptive force of an organization, the force that enables the organization to consciously respond to changed conditions so that it will continue to flourish amidst changes in the market. Being able to adapt to change means leaders must be able to reevaluate their organizations' purpose whenever they become aware that habitual behavior, even if successful to that point, likely will not suffice in the changed climate. Leaders may need to refine, or even redefine, that purpose. When they do, real leaders will act without the security of habitual behavior in the organization. As previously noted, they are the first in an organization willing to step out, to engage in untested behavior and unproven belief. And they, as Quinn says, will "build the bridge as they walk on it." Clarifying purpose and becoming more aware, they can better align their and others' behavior with a jointly held intention that successfully addresses the changing conditions the rapidly approaching future is bringing. They, once again, must step outside the usual boundaries in realignment with a revised or new purpose. Chapter 2 took up the concept of on-purpose leadership in more detail.

Real Leadership: Let's Be Clear

To zero in on what real leadership involves, we need to be clear on what it doesn't. Again, it is not management. To put it more concisely, management controls stasis with quality and consistency—which is essential and which in many ways helps an organization. And change for change's sake is often misguided. An example is J.C. Penney's firing of its CEO in 2013 and the subsequent apology to its established customer base for changing too much too quickly. But when the organization must change—and in the times we live in, this condition has become a virtual guarantee—preserving stasis is counterproductive. Real leadership has to adapt; it has to drive the organization to change. Real leadership is also not politics. Politics involves the art of compromise. Leaders might negotiate, but they do not compromise their purpose or core values. We can see how it's necessary—vividly so in our current society where it is absent between the major political parties. In driving an organization to adapt, however, compromise with regard to the mission or core values is fatal. Altering course for the right reasons may appear to be compromise, but it is radically different. Leaders do the right things to serve the mission, purpose, and core values, not out of fear or political agenda. Real leaders must make sure that everyone in the organization is aware of the purpose, aligned with the purpose, and accountable to the purpose. Moving the organization toward its new purpose leaves no room for compromise on those counts if it is to succeed. Although politics and the compromise therein is a form of human governance, simply put, management and politics do not, in essence, deal with adapting to purpose. Conversely, real leadership is all about adapting.

Now let's look at Purpose and each "A" component (Awareness, Alignment, and Accountability) of the Angel Model in turn, which have all been discussed in more detail in preceding chapters. Then we'll look at how leaders go about transforming their organizations by combining those elements through real leadership, and jumping out of the quit zone.

Before we start, though, here's the Leadership Potential Scale, a set of questions you can answer that will give you insight into how much leadership potential you are using right now. Answer these questions honestly as to how you act now, not how you would like to act. The pattern of your answers will give you an idea of where you can focus to increase effective development of your leadership potential. It often helps to have a trusted partner, customer, or associate to provide a candid assessment. This can further ensure that a blind spot is not blocking that potential.

Leadership Potential Scale

Gain Perspective

1. I know my strengths and weaknesses as well as my ego defensive triggers and defensive behaviors.
2. I can maintain mindfulness in a stressful situation, even when others cannot.
3. I regularly seek feedback to find blind spots. I am transparent and share my views openly.
4. I am mindful and often look ahead to anticipate potential opportunities and problems.
5. I am a student of human behavior and continue to learn about myself and others.
6. I can respectfully listen to others I disagree with to understand each person's point of view.

Act with Courage

7. I hold people accountable even when doing so is unpopular.
8. In the past I have tended to get frustrated by people's inability to perform. I use healthy personal techniques for keeping my stress lowered.
9. I can handle most interpersonal problems in a timely manner should they arise at work.
10. My comfort zone does not dictate my behavior. Purpose and chosen values do.
11. I can manage my emotions so I don't mismanage the people I work with.
12. I can take action without certainty, and consciously hold to my core values.

13. I have changed my life by choice in the past as my old beliefs fought back (at first).
14. I recognize when I am making a decision and taking action based on fear instead of purpose.

Strengthen Integrity

15. I know and use my values and the values of the organization as guides.
16. I make agreements thoughtfully, negotiate cleanly, and keep the agreements I make.
17. Even when someone isn't looking or I wouldn't get caught, I do what is right.
18. I know that what I do to help or hurt another unit of our organization in the long run helps or hurts me.
19. I serve the "enterprise" as well as my specific area of responsibility.
20. I base my thinking on key decisions and actions about what is "on-purpose" for the organization, and what is good for me, others, and the community we serve.

Organizations that promote the development of perspective (self-awareness), courage (accountability), and integrity (alignment) release and focus personal leadership and organizational potential that increases organizational vitality.

Chapter 7
Blind Spots versus Awareness

Most leaders are driving ninety miles per hour down a highway with their windshield blocked and looking in the rearview mirror chanting, "I'm a leader, I'm a leader."

The Johari Window and Blind Spots

An old model that has stood the test of time is the Johari Window. It shows us how human perception is limited by the past and what has been experienced. (See figure 8 for a model I adapted.) In other words, we can't see beyond the limitations of our memory-based beliefs. The Johari Window is brilliantly broken into two general areas of blind spot: what is seen by others that we don't see and what is not seen by others that we do not see, either. The first blind spot is resolved by open communication and "feedback" in a team or in an organization. The second is more difficult and often requires creative, out-of-the-box thinking to engage the more creative parts of ourselves.

This model is instructive. Most of what trips leaders up is not chosen; it is "unknowns"—blind spots and "unknown unknowns," what neither the leader nor associates sees. What is unseen controls the leader and the outcome.

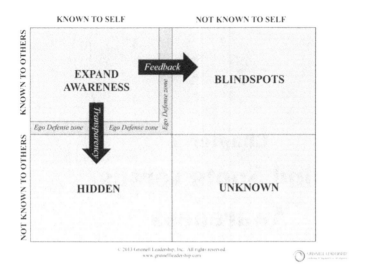

Figure 8. The Johari Window Model (Adapted from Johari Window, Developed by Joseph Luft and Harrington Ingram, Modified for Leadership beyond Belief)

The best ways to shrink blind spots and the unknown unknowns are human beings receiving open, honest feedback and being transparent. This is one of the most significant challenges of the leader: building a culture that supports these behaviors. But for us to expand our awareness zone requires us to go beyond ego or beliefs and our defense mechanisms. This is why self-awareness and knowledge of human nature is so critically important for seeing issues and reaching effective outcomes. Here is how I like to phrase this point:

To get out of the box, you must understand the box.

Human beings stay mired in our old beliefs and perceptions generated by those beliefs and will fight any feedback to the contrary—as long as we are unaware. If you don't know the box, you can't get out of the box. We stay stuck within the limitations of the unaware de-

134

ployment of our ego defense mechanisms as they do their job to protect our ego-identity from being "wrong." Ego doesn't like to be wrong and will resist seeking critical feedback to its idealized view of itself and will often see an imagined transgression. It feels vulnerable and "unsafe" to acknowledge, let alone entertain seriously, a contrary point of view that may mean I will have to change my ways.

To open up and be transparent is a threat as "you may see me contrary to my idealized view, or I think you will use the information to politically hurt me." This is often a form of rationalization for continuing to hide. To go beyond these ego-imposed limitations, to maintain *curiosity* in the face of perceived critical feedback, and to stay conscious while feeling vulnerable constitute the fundamental path to reducing mistakes of leadership. It should be a primary focus of team leadership to create safe environments where people will step out into this new behavior. Admittedly, this takes "stomach," yet is the place the real leader works on himself or herself first, then on the team, and finally on the organization. The work of this chapter is to show you how to go beyond those defense mechanisms and habits so you can see better options, alter course, and adapt to the future successfully. Without this awareness, we are subject to experiencing the unintended consequences of past memory, habits, and beliefs wrongly interacting with conditions a different future brings. Leaders must know this. When old beliefs are brought to a new situation, the key may no longer unlock the door to success.

How Beliefs Form

It's easy to see how beliefs form in our minds. Imagine an Inuit visits you from the frozen North. He has spent his life living in an igloo. You have a mischievous streak and so you've prepared a little demonstration for your guest: you've hung a glass-covered, 12x36 picture on the wall opposite the door in your living room. But this is no ordinary picture: you've rigged it so that when you flip the light switch next to the door, the picture loudly crashes to the floor and shatters into a thousand pieces of glass. The Inuit, quite naturally and reflexively, reacts in a defensive posture. Now, you know that flipping the light switch has no connection to the picture's falling, but the Inuit has never seen either a framed picture or a light switch.

Leadership Beyond Belief

You and your visitor leave the living room—the mess can wait until company leaves—and walk into the adjacent dining room. Sure enough, there is another framed picture on the adjacent wall—though this one is normal—and a light switch next to the door. When you reach out to turn the light switch, the already tense Inuit grabs your arm. What has happened? He has created a belief about a cause and effect—and he's created this belief in one experience, because that experience made such a vivid impression on his mind. As a result of that new belief, he has programmed his mind to associate light switches with danger. As you realize, his belief has nothing to do with reality; it has to do with his experience projected into the unknown future.

If this seems far-fetched, and you're skeptical that we can form a belief based on one event, I'll give you an example from my own experience. My wife and I lived in Japan for several years, and we were about six months into our sojourn, sitting in a restaurant enjoying dinner, when suddenly the Japanese diners screamed and ran for the doors in fear. I noticed that the room seemed to be sliding back and forth, but I didn't have a category for that experience (a belief) and, therefore, couldn't label what was happening or even pretend a response. I had no fear. About the time the sliding stopped I realized, "that was an earthquake!" Six months later, the next time I felt the floor start to slide in Japan, trust me, I felt fear and I scurried. All it took was one experience. This event illustrates dramatically how, without beliefs, we will not survive. It also shows that we not only use them for survival, but they help us make efficient use of our mental and physical attention and energy. Further, beliefs deliver exactly the reflexive and habitual responses they were designed (i.e., learned) for.

Beliefs Run the Organization

Beliefs form in an organization the same way. When you go to work for a company, you are tacitly trained how to act and think within its culture, by people who learned those patterns themselves. They don't really know they are doing it. It's mostly unconscious programming. The systems, processes, and behaviors in the company evolved in response to conditions it faced in the past. Over time, those behaviors become habitual and ingrained. Even before we encounter beliefs formed by individual companies, apprenticing within a specific industry or profession often teaches us to see in a particular way, which was formed in response to conditions within a field in the past—and not necessarily the recent past. Operating out of this mindset frequently causes us to continue to perform actions that are detrimental to our organization's interests under the conditions that exist in that field *now*.

Individual companies develop their own corporate cultures. Beliefs grow out of response to conditions a company faced when it was getting off the ground, and then they become established and often unquestioned, *the way we do things*. Executives support and promote managers who align fully with the old patterns. Managers train new employees how to act and think within the corporate culture. Employees follow them out of habit and they become a routine. The behavior becomes unconscious—and unquestioned. As with an individual's learning to walk or eat, the habitual behaviors save time and energy, and they're not a problem if they still align with the organization's current and future needs. But as with changing channels in an inlet, they can lead to disaster when the company faces a changed environment. When we cling to the wrong beliefs, ones that don't apply to our current situation, we will never reach our potential.

One of the most important things you as a leader can do is understand and watch your own mind so that you can align your behavior with what is right for the organization in the situation at hand. In other words, become self-aware. In doing so, you escape the control of belief. When you become self-aware, you become aware as well of more options and opportunities around you and are able to choose: *you* choose what you should believe, based on current data, and how you should act as a result. If you are unaware of a belief, it will operate perfectly, delivering the outcome and experience it was programmed for until you act to change it. Awareness is the first step.

Leaders need to be aware, too, that organizational and personal beliefs are not necessarily limiting, in a word, negative. Beliefs can be positive, too, as we'll see in the next section. The key, still, is that

Leadership Beyond Belief
leaders need to be aware of what their beliefs are and which ones
work well, in their business and in their lives.

Beliefs are Positive and Productive

Years ago I began coaching a very talented executive, "Jack," who
figuratively went from the "mail room to the board room" within a
very large services company. In the late 1990s he was eventually
challenged with running a one-billion dollar enterprise. As usual he
handled this assignment well and continued to grow the company in
healthy ways. In fact, he told me, he found the role of president to be
more comfortable than any other role he had held yet. That is, he did
until an investor came along and bought the company. This change
brought some nasty politics, played out by some very politically savvy
and power-hungry people Jack had worked with. Many good people
were leveraged out for all the wrong reasons. He told me later that
his quitting was the best move he ever made professionally, as the job
had become much less fun. About six months after he left the company, Jack struck a deal with a large company to start up a regional
office. Soon after the office started, I met him and a couple of his loyal
lieutenants in a hotel room (their first "office")—quite a shift from the
corporate offices we had met in for years.

Amazingly, within about four years the start-up was generating
close to a half billion dollars a year. Within seven years it hit the
billion-dollar mark. It was amazing growth by anyone's standards,
especially in a people-centric services business. So what grew that
company so fast and well? I believe that Jack's talent coupled with
that of other talented leaders who held beliefs formed from already
having successfully led a one-billion dollar company was responsible.
Beliefs they had learned well and embedded into their consciousness
now shaped their perceptions, decisions, and actions at conscious and
unconscious levels and led them back to familiar territory. By the
way, Jack's old company was eventually run into the ground and the
company was taken apart and "sold for scrap."

We often see a similar pattern when a smaller company enters
the fast-growth phase, usually at around a hundred employees. The
ownership (often the founder) will usually begin bringing in people
with larger company experience. This is because the newly hired have

experience and hold beliefs that, not unlike Jack's, allow them to perceive and act in ways befitting a larger enterprise. This is a stumbling point for many owners of small companies, as they see issues and shape solutions from their perspective forged from a start-up and small company experience, and they resist or run the corporate folks away. Those leaders who hire smartly and lead appropriately will usually make their enterprise into a much larger and lucrative affair.

Ego—the Leader's Gift and Nemesis

Human beings are driven by ego. "Having a big ego" actually indicates having a lot of ego *strength*. Ego means "I" in Latin. It is not, however, the "I" that is the true inner self; it is the "I" of the identity. The degree to which you are unaware of how your personality and ego function is the degree to which you are out of control of your outcomes as leader. Without ego strength leaders can't lead; too much drives blind spots and unintended negative consequences. The identity is the picture of yourself that you carry around in your head and that you believe you must live up to at all costs. Your identity (or ego) is a rigid system of belief about yourself that you maintain and reinforce through perception. For example, being "wrong" does not support your view of yourself as "smart" or "competent," and, as a result, you can often argue against ideas, opinions, and even facts to support your ego's idealized view of yourself as being smart and being right (nothing personal here—I've done the same thing in my life; we all have).

You formed this picture of your identity early in life, as a way to cope with the environment you found yourself in. You reinforced it through repeated behavior over the years. Your identity governs how you see, act, and experience yourself in the world. It is an idealized self-image. If this image fits what your life and your leadership require now, then it doesn't cause problems. But if it doesn't fit those needs, it limits you and your organization. To move beyond its limits, you must become aware of that identity from the standpoint of an observer outside the ego, and then change in accord with what your life and your organization currently require for success.

Personality is the outside manifestation of the ego. It's what others experience when they are around you. The personality is what former Harvard professor Richard Alpert, Ph.D., calls "our social space suit." It is the primary tool in leadership, yet most leaders know less about their personality than they do about their profession. Over the years, I've asked thousands of executives a simple question: "What is a personality?" Only a few have been able to answer immediately. When you don't understand your personality, though, it controls you. In fact, the degree to which you are aware is the degree to which you are in control of your leadership outcomes. That which you are unaware of controls you.

The personality helps us meet our social, psychological, spiritual, and physical needs. It is built from one's mind, beliefs, emotions, behavior, and body. The essence of our being is consciousness, aliveness, or, in religious terms, the "soul." But we lose track of this inner essence behind the strength of personality, a word that comes from the Latin word *persona*, referring to an actor's mask. The Romans and before them the Greeks knew that we hide our inner being behind a mask, our personality. This may be the most significant aspect and unique characteristic of our species. We invent a persona, forget it's made up, and live our lives according to that persona, even when it's not working well.

Over time, by paying close attention, we can develop the ability to recognize behavior, thoughts, and perception flowing from our personality. We can then move beyond its constraints to consciousness—of our minds, our emotions, our actions, and where they spring from. Unless we do become aware, we give that automated personality free rein to run our lives.

Here is an example that illustrates how the personality forms at an early age and then dominates our behavior:

Years ago I worked with an executive—let's call him Bob—who was the founder and CEO of a medium-sized software company. He had an IQ of about 150, had a Ph.D. in an area I still can't pronounce, and was very articulate. He had gone to

140

one of the best Ivy League colleges on an academic scholarship. Though his company was successful, once it reached the level of a hundred employees, it could not grow. He hired successful executives from large companies, but in every case he found fault with them—they just couldn't measure up to his standards. Invariably they would eventually quit. Frustrated, he finally began to examine himself. A friend suggested he reach out to us at Grinnell Leadership.

Through the process of self-examination we helped him work through, he came to realize that he was the bottleneck preventing his company from growing. Because he had an overpowering need to be responsible and an overpowering fear of the consequences of failure, he tried to control everything, and even the smallest of issues bothered him. He was unable to distinguish between an important problem and a minor one. He rationalized by blaming the executives who worked for him. His strong intellect and gift of gab enabled him to prevail in every argument; as a result, he eliminated his executives' motivation and caused them to fear him.

The coaching process revealed that Bob had grown up with severely alcoholic parents, who were unable to take care of his younger sister and him. Beginning at the age of six, he had felt an urgent need to grow up so that he could take care of his sister, and try to encourage his mom and dad to get along during their alcoholic tirades. Bob eventually recognized that, in running his company, he felt the same fear he had felt as a child for himself and his sister. After a year of coaching, he gained the perspective on his personality and how it governed his emotions, perceptions, and behavior to stop seeing every minor problem as a life-and-death threat. He went on to change his behavior to the extent that his leadership moved his company to the next level of success.

This example illustrates several important points. First, the ego itself is not the problem. After all, Bob's becoming able to care for himself and his sister was positive. Like beliefs, the ego is essential for survival. But to maintain itself in a challenging world, the ego develops defenses. Deploying those defenses generates automated behavior based on past perceptions and beliefs (at the deepest level, as with Bob, from childhood), and causes a person to attack or withdraw from any input to the personality that doesn't fit what the ego wants to hear. This action of the ego implies the second point: often, as in Bob's case, the most deeply embedded belief is what we call a "false belief": though it was based on perceptions and conditions from long ago, conditions the person confronts now do not conform to those from the past. Bob did not need to "take care of" or overly correct the executives he hired. They could learn from errors and, in large part, perform their own jobs without his control.

Bob could have attended all the best business schools in the world, hired the most experienced executives on the planet, and known his strengths, but until he understood this deeper aspect of his beliefs behind the barrier of awareness, he—like all the rest of us—would continue to be frustrated, chained to the past with false beliefs and thereby unable to access his potential to create the experience he truly wanted.

Defense Mechanisms—"the Great Blinder"

Operating from beliefs, the ego scans the social environment and classifies an event, a comment, or a person in that environment as either a threat or not a threat. When something happens or something is said that doesn't support the ego's idealized image in the identity, it responds defensively. Often that response is inappropriate to the current situation. For instance, a leader may react to a minor accounting error or a small mistake a subordinate has made as though a saber-tooth tiger was attacking (I'll get back to that image—it's important). This reaction is part of what we can call a "sucker's choice": it gives a short-term emotional release, but produces a long-term damaged relationship, leads to repeated bad patterns, and reduces trust and respect.

The ego has a variety of defense mechanisms it can call up when it feels threatened; here are a few of the more common ones we see in organizations:

- *Rationalization*: used when we are confronted with points of view that are contrary to what we believe. As we saw with Bob, he rationalized as incompetence those perspectives and actions that were different from his own. Rationalizing enables the ego to maintain its sense of competence.

- *Denial*: an extreme form of rationalization. It motivates someone to avoid considering new information that does not fit into the perceptual patterns of the past. The severe case is that of a narcissistic leader who is unable to examine his or her own behavior and so avoids personal or organizational feedback for fear of not looking good, a perception that would not meet the idealized self-image. Less severe, but still dangerous, is the "sunny-side-up" leader, who wants to keep peace at any price. For example, some parents will not see their teenagers using drugs because it would be so difficult first to acknowledge and second to deal with; the situation doesn't fit their idealized family picture.

- *Pleasing*: unlike denial, comes into play when a leader sees the issues, but will not take the required actions to deal with them because those actions might displease others. Pleasers want everyone to like them and feel very anxious at the least resistance or negative feedback. The ego perceives such feedback as meaning "I'm not likeable."

- *Withdrawing and withholding*: not saying something we think is important because of a real—or often fantasized—fear of repercussion, political or otherwise. Most of us are familiar with this mechanism. Our belief may not allow us to see ourselves as being as smart or experienced as the other people in the room or we may be reluctant to speak because we fear embarrassing the boss or a colleague. This mechanism contributes to a culture of fear of blame and mistake, which can be deadly to an organization trying to react to new conditions.

- *Stonewalling*: refraining from saying something we think is important, not out of fear, but out of anger. A colleague who's stonewalling will smile and nod, but on the inside be steamed. Ultimately, the steam has to release, and the "stonewaller" will ventilate, attacking with contrary perspectives or actions (usually behind the scenes and one's back), which is self-defeating for the leader and for the organization.

- *Winning the argument*: "I'm right, you're wrong." People using this defense feel threatened if they can't perceive themselves as smart or as a winner. If they combine high IQ and an ability to articulate, they can "win" the argument—on the surface. Over time, however, people around them stop sharing information and perspectives, a prescription for their growing blind spots with eventual failure and a potential organizational catastrophe.
- *Sarcasm*: an indirect way of communicating frustration at a person or situation. Others perceive sarcasm as criticism, so it erodes trust and reduces the flow of information. Both are essential to coping with new conditions.

To construct a flowchart of your own behavior, examine the reasons for your reactions, perceptions, and feelings, digging back into your past—back to your childhood—to search for the events, the situations, the people that led you to form your personality the way you did. What self-defense mechanisms does *your* ego typically employ? Do they look like something your mom or dad or whoever raised you deployed? Are they different at home and at work? Don't look at the people around you now to explain the way you act now; look at yourself.

A model I developed years ago I've found helpful for understanding how the mind operates and causes us to behave is the Defensiveness Model (figure 9). It makes clear how information flows through the perceptual filter we erect from our emotional responses or styles like some of those above. If you become aware of the elements of your filter through which information flows, you are better able to keep that filter cleaner, so to speak, so that your perceptions occur in the neutral zone rather than immediately being shunted to the defensive zone.

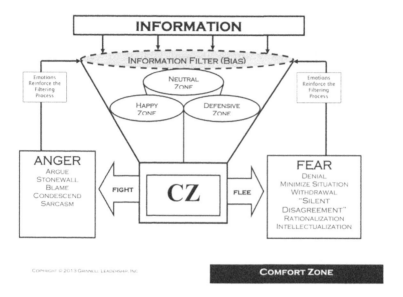

Figure 9. The Defensiveness Model for Explaining How Defensiveness Arises to Protect the Ego-Identity and the Status Quo

Awareness of our defensive style is useful for disengaging it, which helps the leader gather more information for better decisions and actions. When information is shared the ego (identity) or idealized self-image responds to it in three possible ways.

The "happy zone" response is when the information fits the idealized self-image of the leader. It feels like a "compliment" to what one likes to think about oneself. This is usually not a problem and should be enjoyed. Defense mechanisms are not usually deployed in this situation. Second is the "neutral zone" response whereby the leader doesn't really care one way or the other. It is like "water off a duck's back" and doesn't elicit a defensive or overly happy response—more of a neutral response. Again, defensive behavior is not deployed here. The third potential response is a "defensive zone" response. In this case the information is perceived as a threat to the idealized self-image, and the ego responds by deploying defense mechanisms to justify, withdraw, or attack. When leaders unconsciously deploy defensive zone responses they create unconscious and often conscious fear in others with whom they work, who thereby block the flow of information to them. This is critical because without accurate, timely, and useful information the leader and the area he or she is responsible for is much more vulnerable and likely to create a negative unintended consequence via blind spot protected by a defense mechanism.

Curiosity—the Ego's Antivenom

Consider another scenario:

A very bright entrepreneur loved what he did; the success of the company he founded showed that clearly. But for three of the past five years, his business had stalled at $2.5 million in revenue; no matter how hard he tried, he couldn't get the company to grow beyond that point. He knew he had to do something different and, since he was the entrepreneur, he hired an experienced manager who had developed infrastructure to support rapid growth in several other companies, and the two began expanding the business. Revenues grew quickly.

But the CEO became uncomfortable. Feeling left out of the middle of the action in the company, even though they had clarified roles, he came to believe he was not pulling his weight in the firm. He missed having people come to him, seeking his advice. His contact with his manager diminished and he began to go around her to offer guidance. Sometimes that advice ran counter to her initiatives. She began to confront him about his "nonsupportive behavior." When she did, he reacted defensively and withdrew.

Now the CEO's stomach began to bother him, which was surprising for someone who had bragged for years about being able to eat or drink anything. The growth he had wanted for so long was coming at a price he didn't know he would have to pay; the payment came in the form of lingering discomfort that affected not just his stomach but his ability to experience satisfaction and joy.

Blind Spots versus Awareness

I mentioned earlier that personality is built not only from beliefs, perceptions, and behavior but from the body as well. This is important to keep in mind, because the body is affected when the ego exercises its defenses. Bodily reactions are signals, and one aspect of developing self-awareness is recognizing what those signals are communicating. If this CEO had been more aware of how his personality caused him to act, he would have understood that the physical and emotional discomfort he experienced was telling him something.

A more self-aware entrepreneur would have admitted that the discomfort sent up a red flag about his reaction to change. An honest self-examination might have led him to understand the cause of his behavior and to realize that it was undercutting someone who was trying to help him. When we go beyond our egos, and the habitual behaviors and perceptions they drive, we often find that change is necessary—and change makes us uncomfortable. When we start to act in new ways, counter to our habitual practice, we encounter "the dragon."

The Dragon's Fire

Personality helps us get our physical, emotional, and self-esteem needs met so we can feel stable and survive, but it is also an ego dragon that stands guard for the ego, protecting habitual beliefs, perceptions, and behavior that the ego has built over time. Metaphorically, the dragon's fire is that emotional and physical discomfort we feel when change threatens those habitual practices. The dragon roars if you try to move away from them; it responds to threats to the identity that the ego has constructed for you. Unlike St. George, you cannot slay the dragon to rid your life of its fire. What you can do is examine, understand, and befriend the dragon, and turn it from guardian of your ego into a guide helping you and others toward purpose directed by chosen values.

Breaking free of blind spots, denial, and the fear of change is not easy. It is uncomfortable. Being honest with yourself can be painful when you dig deeply into experiences early in your life in order to recognize and reconstruct what lies at the foundation of your personality and the perceptions and reactions its beliefs create. Bright, capable people who get fired or demoted or who just do not reach their potential tend to hit an emotional sticking point, then they block self-awareness and lose perspective. Not moving past that point prevents them from seeing how they have contributed, at least in part, to the undesirable outcomes they experience. You must go through that discomfort and pain the ego generates to reach a better place. If you can't see how your behavior springs from your personality's perceptions and beliefs, particularly false and misaligned beliefs, you cannot choose a better course. You first need to be honest with yourself, and recognize and understand the beliefs, judgments, perceptions, and resulting behavior that produce unsatisfying outcomes.

Once you understand them, you have to accept responsibility—an important step in human growth and leadership development. In other words, stop blaming others and seeing yourself as a victim. We can avoid the dragon's fire by justifying our actions with familiar rationalizations that prove us right and reassure us we have no reason to change. This is the reflexive path. Or we can acknowledge that bad things do happen to people and organizations, but that we have a choice in how we respond to them.

We have seen in our work over the years that everyone makes mistakes or gets negative feedback at times in their careers. What the real leaders, young or old, seem to do is hurt for a bit, then pick themselves up by the bootstraps and figure out how to solve the problem. They don't get caught in blame or finger-pointing for very long before they figure out how to move on creatively to reach their purpose. In other words, we can meet the challenge and lead, or we can stay in our familiar unaware state and play victim.

Mastering Your Dragon

When you've recognized your behavioral patterns and taken full responsibility for them, you then must choose new behaviors, focused on the outcome you want. You may need to ask others for advice here, certainly must bounce them against your core values; sometimes blind spots keep us from seeing a better alternative. After you identify a better course and choose to pursue it, you enter the dragon's lair. Up to this point in your life, the ego has automatically managed your behavior and helped you achieve your current level of

148

success. If you consciously change your behavior, the dragon awakens and breathes the fire of emotional discomfort. The dragon stands guard at the entrance to the cave where the ego dwells, keeping things consistent, fighting adaptation, causing us to continue in the same patterns.

Riding the Dragon®

Many people meet the dragon, but most continue their old patterns to avoid the discomfort that disrupting them brings. Few have the courage to ride the dragon. To make your life better, and to become a better leader, you must feel the dragon's emotional fire and not shove it back down into the body through repression or denial. To ride the dragon, you don't ignore the emotion, you accept it. When you sense that it's telling you how to act in the old familiar way, however, you choose to act differently, to follow the new action directed at a different outcome. You act "on-purpose."

A Personal Example of Riding My Dragon

At just the wrong time in a rather important meeting two phones went off. The worst part was that one of them was mine. Immediately feeling *embarrassed* I scrambled to turn it off, but before I could do so the meeting leader mentioned it and I *felt* caught. My habitual response in this type of situation is to feel an uncomfortable tension in my gut and chest. Then my mind and mouth quickly come to the rescue by creating conceptual frameworks and words to explain why it was "not my fault." I might say, "You don't understand and I was not wrong" or "You were wrong and here's why." However, this time, instead of reacting, I just watched and didn't execute my rationalizations; I put them aside and continued to experience what was going on *inside me.*

I observed that as the guilt and shame, and my resulting need to rationalize, subsided, they were replaced by feelings of anger and self-righteousness. I continued to observe my feelings and not to speak out. It was a small thing, but I merely paid attention to my emotions, my body, and my mind and to what they did. To my surprise, a subtle

149

yet significant insight eventually showed through like a brilliant green daffodil tip breaking ground in early spring. I saw *experientially* that all the self-justification and rationalization I had done over the years was an aggressive act. It was not consciously intended, but, still, it was truly aggressive. This time, behind my ego defense I felt a peacefulness and I further understood that I had worked too hard and had done too much to protect my identity over the years.

Please don't get me wrong—I understand the need for creating boundaries, and how anger and all the associated behaviors of rationalization and self-justification can protect us. *Yet how often do leaders unnecessarily justify and rationalize to alleviate their emotional discomfort with their associates, customers, and patients and, as an unintended consequence, put boundaries between themselves and the people they rely on for trust, respect, information, collaboration, and success?*

This example may be simple, but it is not simplistic; it is deceptively important. It is the process by which leaders develop perspective and move beyond the boundaries of the defense-laden protection of their past beliefs and behaviors to create new and different outcomes—one day, one conversation, one experience at a time. Whether it is launching a new strategy or sitting in a meeting, as I was, it is the same simple, but often most difficult thing to do: pay attention and ride the dragon instead of reacting from a defensive past.

Embrace Your Ego Dragon, Don't Fight It

In part, riding the dragon involves continuing with your chosen new behavior, focused on your desired outcome. Riding the dragon also involves a physical reaction. Remember the example of reacting to a minor problem as though a saber-tooth tiger were attacking? That reaction is a relic of our prehistoric days as a species, when physical danger would arouse our limbic system to a "fight-or-flight" response. We needed this kind of response to survive, whether the danger we faced was from a wild animal or from a human adversary.

Now, however, although we seldom experience extreme danger, the limbic system still operates in times of stress. Stress triggers the limbic system to respond with the same fight-or-flight feeling. Most of the time that response is unnecessary and experiencing it a lot, as many of us do in our stressful lives, is physiologically unhealthy. It also reduces our ability to think effectively and solve problems. The example of my "overreaction" when the ringing phone interrupted the meeting vividly illustrates these points.

When I lived in Japan, I studied martial arts. My sword teacher taught me a simple technique, one used in Japanese martial arts for centuries. It has served as a valuable tool for me and for many people I have coached over the years, helping them go beyond their current behavioral boundaries. I call it "2X breathing," and just as it sounds, it involves breathing twice as long. More specifically, to practice this technique, you inhale and then exhale, taking twice as long to exhale as you do to inhale. This breathing is not exaggerated; you breathe as you normally would—or would when you're not stressed, that is—and exhale easily. At the same time as you're following this breathing pattern, you focus your awareness on the place in your body where you feel the discomfort. Often when we experience stress, we'll feel a physical symptom—a discomfort in the stomach or a rising anxiety in the head. Wherever that discomfort is, focus your awareness on it and breathe in the 2X pattern.

With conscious relaxation and 2X breathing in the face of the dragon's fire, along with moving forward with new behavior, you begin to shift your body into accepting the new pattern. It may take one time or five times or five hundred times of repeating this technique, but if you maintain your resolve and continue on your course, you will experience a physical change. Each time you react in this way to the dragon's fire, you signal your limbic system that this new behavior is *different but not dangerous*. As this shift occurs, you are on your way to making the dragon your guardian, helping sustain new behavioral patterns that lead to greater success and satisfaction.

The 2X breathing technique is one of three ways of centering yourself that grew out of ancient martial arts. A second, which I learned from Dr. Gerald Hutchison, is "embrace and surrender." As you inhale slowly and gently, but deeply (though without filling your lungs entirely), embrace in your mind the creation of the present moment as it is as part of God's work, if you are spiritually inclined, or else as the unfolding of destiny created by your actions and those of others in the past. Embrace your ego's need to be in control (again, don't repress it). Embrace yourself in trust that you can figure a creative way to solve the problem at hand.

As you exhale slowly and gently, surrender yourself to that moment, to God's plan or to destiny. Surrender your ego's need to control. Surrender your ideas about how things have to turn out. Be aware that the moment is what it is and that you can't change the past. You can only go forward and solve the problem.

The third practice is "real-time centering." Though it originated in Asian martial arts and yoga, a great deal of Western medical research at the Heart Math Institute supports the positive effects of this process: improved pulse rate and rhythm, blood pressure, and immune response. You can do this technique with your eyes open if need be, but it's more effective with eyes closed. First, start 2X breathing, as described here. Then, imagine breathing in a crystal clear blue sky. Remember a moment when you were serene, and how you felt then. As you exhale, imagine sending out that feeling as if you were passing it on to someone else. Be aware of your body's relaxing. Then repeat the process. The Heart Math Institute conducts training programs on a process similar to real-time centering.

This process is one you can carry with you and use on the spot when you need to rapidly lead the stress in your body to subside. It will help you gain greater poise and think more effectively as you make your decisions as a leader.

Building Your Observer-Operator with Awareness

In some of our workshops we use another process to help our clients understand what awareness is. We have participants sit quietly and just notice their breathing, body sensations, mind, and emotions. The part that watches is the reflective or "aware" part of consciousness. The minute we form a judgment, label, or position in our mind about the object of consciousness, we are back in the memory-based zone again. Just watching, noticing, however, is almost like being an explorer walking in an area you have walked through a hundred times, but while being awake for the first time. There is no prejudgment or pretense, just observation and unlabeled experience.

Blind Spots versus Awareness

This place of observation and experience in consciousness deepens with time. It is one of the goals of meditation: to gain control of your mind and its habitual wanderings by letting go of control and by just observing. When you realize that you are back in judgment and thinking mode you just notice and bring yourself back to awareness. If you judge yourself you just notice the judgment—some people like to just name it "judgment"—and move back to noticing what is going on here and now. Some people use their breath and the movement of their body to recenter on the present, on their bodies as they breathe or on the sensation of the cool air going in and out of their noses, to focus on what is happening now.

It is the practice of bringing yourself back to awareness of the here and now. Success is not sitting in a lotus position with a guru in some faraway place and studying with a master to learn these techniques. That exotic journey, of course, is one way to do it, but the other way is to do it "in the marketplace." Moment by moment during the endless meetings we hold in our businesses is a great place to practice being awake. And when you do, you may also find that you will see things and understand things in ways you haven't before, while strapped into your memory-based belief system.

As we slow down a bit, and are able to look from a more aware place, most of us begin to notice patterns that have dictated the current outcomes in our life and leadership. Peter Senge, founder of the Society for Organizational Learning at MIT, in a wonderful CD he published several years ago actually recommends that we slow down. Altering the rhythm of our life will awaken us, he tells us. He suggests walking slower, responding slower, breathing a bit slower, and so on in order to learn to stay awake. This practice is very powerful. Ironically, "to go slow to go fast" is so true when it comes to leadership, and the ability to find new paths and to summon ample courage to lead change.

Awareness comes on at least two levels. There may be many more, but for leaders, there are two significant levels. First, there is the level that "*I am my mind.*" That is, I am my thoughts, beliefs, reactions, emotions, and so on, which are dictated by my "nature." This is in part true, but this kind of awareness ignores the fact that experiences create memory-based beliefs that guide perception, decisions (conscious and unconscious), and action. At this level the individual leader is completely out of control, reacting to an existing programming he or she doesn't acknowledge. This leader's life is like being on a railroad track with one destination. Often when the situation changes, these leaders will continue to do what they have always done and end up creating unintended negative outcomes due to their lack of awareness.

The second level is *"I have a mind,* but I am not my mind." At this level the leader acknowledges a consciousness outside his or her beliefs, precepts, concepts, and interpretations. Jim Farr (1994) points out that such a leader has more control of the personal and organizational outcomes than the first type. These leaders are able to look ahead, and create choices and behaviors in alignment with the future they want to create—in large part the level of consciousness this book advises, the level at which leaders are aware that their beliefs and perceptions are memory-based and have nothing to do with either right now or the future. Those who primarily operate at the second level (I have a mind) tend to be less victimized by circumstances and can take an innovative stand to create in a changing future—if they have the courage to do so.

The more our awareness or free consciousness evolves, the more we can see other options. Milton Erickson says, "He who has the most options wins." What he means by this is that through the process of not reacting in a habitual manner, and by staying awake, we can learn new ways of seeing, being, and doing. In line with Erickson's comment, I like to say that "the leader who has the most options wins." In other words, the leader who is not awake will default to previous memory-based conclusions and reactions, and may not be able to creatively address the fast-approaching future. This process of evolving one's awareness of options is not easy work; the ego, identity, and memory will fight with strong defense mechanisms, trying to bring a familiar stasis to an ever-changing universe of possibilities.

The Next Step: Mindfulness in the Marketplace

One of the wonderful things about the martial arts is that it teaches the student to "be present" while in motion or in action dealing with whatever situation is encountered. This is an exact metaphor for a leader's operating from a place of consciousness and free intelligence. In the martial arts, if your attention wanders and you are not present while sparring, you will get hit. In business, we may be following out of habit policies or standard operating procedures exactly as they are designed, and we may feel safe, but as even one factor changes, the reflexive response may, in fact, become the problem and, instead of our getting hit, the enterprise, and perhaps a career, takes a hit. When you are in leadership, conditions are constantly changing; whether you are addressing a migrating market or dishing out an assignment in a manner that engages followers' motivations, these tasks require consciousness—being present—to be done well.

Mindfulness is simply noticing what is going on right now, paying full attention to what you are doing. Being in the here and now does not mean avoiding planning. It means that, while we are planning, we are fully present doing so. As George Leonard told me years ago at the Esalen Institute in Big Sur, California, by mindfulness we are enabled to "taste the life we are given." Our taste buds in this context are free consciousness or awareness, unbound by beliefs.

While it is helpful to have an understanding of the origins of our egos, we can spend too much time looking back, overanalyzing the past, as well as worrying about the future. To live in the moment is to surrender a great deal of attachment to outcomes (while continuing to work diligently to achieve them). To be mindful is to be fully and completely in the moment with what we are doing, thinking, or saying. Over time, this practice will result in greater focus, peacefulness, and conscious choice to create a desired outcome.

After studying Aikido for many years, I got a job working for the Japanese government to study with true masters of the art. While in Japan, my wife and I were invited to study a not-well-known martial art called Iaido. It consists of certain specific, incredibly detailed and precise movements done with the intention of perfection, all the way down to the minutest details of finger positions, foot positions, swing angles, and so on. The level of detail is truly amazing and requires great focus and concentration, so much so that if your mind wanders there is no way you will be successful at completing the prescribed movements. We were in an unheated dojo during the winters in Okazaki, Japan, yet after only a few minutes in this ice-cold place, we were strangely sweating. The sweat was the result of the required concentration coupled with slow deliberate movements of the body—with complete awareness. For me this was truly a mindfulness practice, using the activity of Iaido as the focus of an active meditation.

Most of this book focuses on giving readers a language and a model for understanding their existing beliefs and how those beliefs drive outcomes. More importantly, the intent is to give you as the leader more control of your mind so that you can create intended outcomes and avoid the unintended ones. It is also precisely attuned to the concept of making conscious choices about our values so we can get the life we want rather than continuing to operate by the false ones that limit our potential. But what do we do once we are aware and know there is a place "beyond belief"?

For most people, the challenge of meditating or maintaining mindfulness in a cave is not a path we would choose. Many of us may even know the benefits of meditation, but we are just more interested in our lives of work, family, and whatever adventure we are on. This is why the path of mindfulness was first developed as a way for people to learn to focus and control their mind "in the marketplace." It is probably much more difficult outside a monastery, but this is the busy path that many of us are designed for.

First, mindfulness is, as previously mentioned, "just noticing" what is going on "right now." It may be that I am noticing as I am typing this part of my book the sounds of the keyboard as I type. It could be watching the letters scroll onto the screen as I type. As I do it I am fully present. But the most important thing I have found in mindfulness work is noticing when I am *not* doing it and bringing myself back to waking consciousness. Noticing when I am not doing it and then bringing myself back to noticing what is going on right now, inside or outside myself, is, in fact, the practice of mindfulness. Many

156

people, in my experience, feel like failures when they notice that they are not fully present, but that is not the case. When you notice that you are no longer present, perhaps daydreaming or worrying, just gently say "thank you" (to the part that woke you up) and ease back into the awareness of the *here* and fully experience what you are doing now. Over time, your mind will begin to focus for longer periods.

An important practice of mindfulness is listening—without a doubt the most important leadership skill (see Tom Peters on listening YouTube video). To pay attention through fully listening not only is a way to gather the information you need, but to listen without judging when what someone says is against your beliefs becomes a powerful gift. Entering very difficult and emotion-laden situations, the one who can truly and calmly be present and listen, instead of going into ego defenses, can often provide the equanimity needed for a better resolution. For me, listening has been my "here and now" meditative practice. Most of the success I enjoy has come because I am pretty much a blank slate when I listen to a client's problems and create solutions based on what I hear, now, instead of from past solutions or interpretations. This holds true for leaders in general: leaders who first hear and then see their followers for who they really are, with perception undistorted by the barrier of personality, can cause much more followership.

Have you ever just stopped and looked around? An example of when I did this once was while I was waiting for my son during a tutoring session at the Open Eye Café in Chapel Hill. It was a beautiful, blue-skied, cloudless, seventy- degree day. I realized that I was in my head, not noticing anything except irrelevant mind chatter. I stopped, paid attention to my breath, and just looked without judgment or attachment to anything around me. I saw the name of the store across the street, the trees, a sign, and many other things I had completely missed when I was unconscious. When I only observe, I am present, but the minute I start judging or analyzing, thinking "this or that is good or bad, tasteful, distasteful, ugly, pretty" and on and on, I am back in what Asians call "the monkey mind," jumping from one tree to the other and missing the unfolding of life around me.

Leadership Beyond Belief

We all have a lifetime, but we can only live, truly live, in this one moment; there is no past—it is only memory. There is only an imagined future, imaged from memory. We can only truly live in the moment, and the savvy leader takes full advantage of this, using free consciousness to listen deeply, to pay attention, and over time to learn to recalibrate his or her stress response.

Maria Gonzalez (2012) in her book *Mindful Leadership* shares research that finds significant gains in physical and emotional health can take place as a result of mindfulness practice. She goes through pages of reported research showing its benefits, such as lowering blood pressure, reducing anxiety, and improving sleep.

Mindfulness is the everyday practice of "just noticing." It becomes a basis for real dialogue and the suspension of belief discussed in chapter 4. It is the process by which, over time, we gain control of the mind and its memory, full of the beliefs that often automate our lives. With purpose as one's guide, from a place of mindfulness it becomes much easier to see the forest for the trees and take right action, as being mindful tends to reduce our attachment to past approaches unless these approaches are still useful in the present.

Appendix 3 contains a wonderful process for meditation, the best I have seen. I began using it over twenty years ago. Meditation for just a few minutes throughout the day, or for extended periods, is mindfulness practice. The thing to know is that for many of us just "chopping wood and carrying water" in the marketplace is a great teacher if we are mindful while we chop and carry, pay attention to what we're doing, and thus choose to use that teacher.

Suggestions for Being Mindful in the Marketplace

Here are some steps you can take to increase your mindfulness as a leader.

1. Use the "Ride the Dragon®" technique when anticipating or going through an emotionally challenging situation.
2. Obtain a copy of Peter Senge's (2009) two-CD set *The Power of Presence* on the Sounds True label. Listen to it a number of times and follow his recommendations.

158

3. Practice mindfulness. When you notice that you are unaware of what is going on around and inside of you, slow down, breathe, and notice what is happening. No matter what activity you are doing, just pay attention to it and notice. Read George Leonard's book *Mastery*.
4. Read Maria Gonzalez's book *Mindful Leadership*.
5. Read the meditation guidelines in appendix 3.
6. Listen more, talk less. Notice when you are thinking about what is being said, instead of working to understand what the other person's position is.
7. Take up a "traditional" art such as yoga, Aikido, Iaido, or tai chi, with the intention of doing it with mindfulness.
8. Remember, success in practicing mindfulness is not based on being calm and centered. Success is any time you notice you are unaware and running on your automatic, reflexive mind, then stop and breathe yourself back to center.

Moving Forward

When you choose to move forward with new behavior, riding the dragon and transforming it from the guard of your ego to the guardian of yourself and your intentions, and becoming more aware, you can use some practical techniques to help you move. First, though, I would encourage you to find an organization or a personal coach with experience in guiding people through the process of self-awareness in a business context. Companies and individuals who engage in this work often advertise their services as "leadership development." Books can help (keep reading!), but they are no substitute in the long run for a coach who has years of firsthand experience helping people with the process.

Furthermore, you need to make a long-term commitment. A weekend program might help you start the process, but becoming self-aware to the point of turning your life and your business in a new direction takes time. Keep in mind, too, that you should not compartmentalize self-awareness: this process of transformation is not just for your career, it's for all areas of your life—your home life and your relationships with those close to you.

If you lead an organization, train your key leaders in being self-aware. You want to weave agility, creativity, and focused motivation into the fabric of your organization. Self-awareness won't tell you the right thing to do in any situation. But in leading, it helps you to recognize what is not consciousness (the automated habitual behavior with its limited outcomes) and creates an opening in the mind. By focusing your consciousness on that opening, you become aware of those limitations and the options for alternatives. There are techniques, such as those already discussed, to help you carry out alternative patterns of behavior.

Once Aware, Become Responsible

An important step in growing capacity for change as a leader is taking responsibility—choosing to solve problems and not act defensively. Leaders are going to get negative feedback. They're going to feel hurt, angry, scared, embarrassed, and disappointed. Being responsible as a leader means not wallowing in those feelings that negative feedback can provoke. Daniel Goleman of Harvard University has conducted research on a concept he discusses in his book *Emotional Intelligence.* He refers to emotional intelligence as "EQ," and finds that organizational insight and effectiveness as a leader does not spring necessarily from a high IQ, but rather from self-awareness, the ability to monitor one's own mind, emotions, and belief-based perceptions. EQ, in fact, is one of the key reasons people move from the mail room to the boardroom, Goleman argues. A successful business leader must have a strong ego to fuel the drive and ambition to succeed. But such a leader must also have a strong EQ, the ability to manage strong, often painful emotions while remaining focused on the task at hand. The responsible leader will refuse to play the victim amid negative feedback, but will consider various options without feeling wrong, incompetent, or unintelligent. These leaders stay at choice and on-purpose within emotionally challenging situations.

Becoming aware is the first step. I can be aware of my anger and still blame you for it and nothing will change for me, or those who work with me. My leadership will not improve. But after you become aware of the off-purpose pattern of behavior, the second step of accepting responsibility for your actions, feelings, and perceptions is the step for beginning change. One coaching assignment we had years ago points this out vividly:

Our team worked with a New York construction executive we will name Joe. He tended to get angry when people disregarded his directions or disagreed with him. When he attended our four-day intensive group coaching clinic, he finally realized that as long as he continued to think others were the cause of his anger, he was enslaved by his perceptions, waiting for others to change their behavior. The "ah-ha" moment for him came at a session where I raised both thumbs and asked the group what that gesture meant. Most, who were from North America, said it meant "right on" or "good job." I pointed out that in other cultures, this same gesture means something very different and it makes people angry. At that moment, Joe realized he was creating his own anger and that as long as he saw the cause of it as other people's behavior, he was going to be stuck with the negative outcomes his anger produced. He understood that, while other people might act in certain ways, he was responsible for his reactions, which were rooted in his habitual beliefs that drove his reflexive response, and not in others' actions.

At a follow-up planning meeting I attended, another executive said something that seemed to irritate him and he characteristically started turning red. Everyone knew the explosion was coming next. The other leader said good-naturedly, "Joe, it looks like we're pissing you off again." He turned and looked at me and winked. "No," he said, "I am pissing on myself." The others rolled with laughter. What I knew in that moment was he was very likely to change. Over time, he did change his behavior, and he began to achieve the outcomes he wanted. He was no longer acting as an angry victim, blaming others. Instead he solved problems.

Going beyond Team-Based Limitations

When you take creative action, you try new approaches and implement different behavior. This practice can be valuable in raising to the surface beliefs that have been automating behavior that you still are not aware of, even though you've started moving toward self-awareness. Sometimes they haven't been relevant in your life or business, but may nonetheless control future behavior. When I launched my consulting business over twenty years ago, it was something I had a strong desire to do. Yet when I borrowed $50,000 to start it, I began to feel strong anxiety, which sometimes moved into panic. I had been successful in the same work, with a company owned by someone else, so I had no negative experience that should have caused me such anxiety. When I engaged in some inner work to gain insight into my reaction, I finally discovered a controlling belief that had lain dormant when I worked for others, but that emerged the minute I took the leap.

My mother comes from a very successful line of entrepreneurs. My great-grandfather succeeded to a high degree and others continued the success. In the process, our family created a myth of success that was passed on to me. So when I began my own business, I believed that my identity as an entrepreneur and as a "Kline" (my mother's maiden name) was at risk if I did not succeed. I kept going though, and the company has operated successfully ever since that beginning many years ago. Humans often avoid testing the validity of their fear. And if I hadn't worked to become aware and if I hadn't taken creative action moving forward, I never would have known whether I could succeed or not and would never have lived my chosen life.

Understanding Others

Being aware of yourself is the most important form of awareness; it's the essential first step for becoming a real leader. But being aware of others and the ways they think and act, and why they think and act in those ways, is necessary too. The ego's defense mechanisms

Blind Spots versus Awareness

covered earlier—pleasing, stonewalling, and the others—are important to know in understanding yourself. They're instructive in understanding others as well. If you understand how they cause people to behave and why, you can better control your reactions and more likely will be better able to predict how people will act and react, and also what is likely to motivate them.

Other, more detailed ways of understanding other people are available. The next chapter will go into detail about how to read or "understand" other people's personalities as well as their psychological and social needs to create what I call "need-goal alignment." Need-goal alignment is the foundation of deftly marshaling the motivations of others toward a leader's objectives. For now though, here are some ways you can involve those you work with to begin to understand how each other "ticks," and thereby begin to align team members' strengths with their roles.

In our consulting work we use the Myers-Briggs Type Indicator (MBTI) to discern personality types, and other instruments as well, which provide similar profiles, but from different perspectives. The Personality Research Form E (PRF-E) is an instrument that you will need to be trained to use. It identifies personality characteristics based on twenty traits such as achievement, affiliation, and impulsivity. A high score in achievement, for example, would indicate someone who is driven to complete challenging tasks. A high score in the cognitive structure factor would indicate someone who wants to base decisions on definite knowledge and likes things "black and white" and dislikes ambiguity. Again, knowing the characteristics and their implications for human behavior can be a valuable source of awareness about why you yourself and those you work with—and live with—act the ways they do.

Many professional coaches use the FIRO-B, which stands for Fundamental Interpersonal Relations Orientation–Behavior, with executives, and it is another instrument we use in our work. The FIRO-B assesses interpersonal needs of individuals, grouped into "expressed" and "wanted" needs for inclusion, control, and affection. For instance, the scores on the combined factors of control indicate whether a person prefers to control others or be controlled. The instrument gives an indication of how individuals are likely to form

Leadership Beyond Belief

relationships. A high score in both expressed affection and wanted affection, for example, indicates someone who likes people and wants to avoid rejection to such a degree that he or she is driven to be well liked and to avoid criticizing—who, in other words, may be a pleaser.

Personality profiles from such instruments are based on decades of exhaustive research. Understanding various temperaments, in as much detail as you can, and how they likely play out in the workplace gives you useful insight—in a word, *awareness*. One way we can break down personality types as they manifest in the workplace is depicted in figure 10. Knowing how various MBTI types see the world, what motivates them, and how frequent they are among people is a tool for increasing awareness, again of both yourself and others. A great deal of information on character traits and how they interact as revealed in the various instruments mentioned is extensive; I can only touch on it here. These instruments are a starting point that begins the process of becoming self-aware.

But deep self-awareness comes from learning to observe yourself and learn in the real time of your daily life and leadership. The more awareness you can gain through these kinds of instruments or other means regarding how others think and behave, and the beliefs and personality traits behind their thoughts and actions, the better prepared you'll be to go about the work of aligning them (as well as yourself) with the mission and goals of the organization, as we'll discuss in the next chapter.

	Pragmatic	Affiliator
Concrete-Real	Stabilizer-Administrator (over 60% of population) Driven to maintain stability, predictability, and control Patient, reliable, follows through Learns step by step, systematically Can place too much emphasis on risk management and jump to conclusions too easily	Troubleshooter-Artisan (over 30% of population) Driven to be responsible, flexible, and practical Acts practically without delay, endures, loyal, clever in addressing problems Learns hands-on, through experience Can procrastinate, operates tactically rather than strategically, may not follow policy and take too many risks
Abstract-	Rationalist-Architect	Idealist-Catalyst

164

Symbolic	(about 4–6% of population)	(about 2–3% of population)
	Driven to experiment to gain knowledge, turns complexity to simplicity, achieves big mission	Driven to inspire others with vision of possibility
	Thinks strategically, thinks in terms of systems, ingenious	Charismatic, passionate, insightful about others, thinks outside the box
	Learns by following interests and examining concepts behind facts	Learns by collaborating with others
	Can be intolerant of redundancy, nit-picks, finds personal concerns irrelevant and can be aloof	Can burden self with the workload, emotional and moralistic, can play favorites and have trouble with criticism
		Natural empathy, overly pleasing, slow to be critical of others unless stressed
		Politically savvy

Figure 10. Guide to MBTI Temperaments (Based on *Please Understand Me* by David Keirsey and Marilyn Bates [1978])

Changing Course

Becoming aware is important throughout life for personal happiness as well as work success, but it's perhaps even more critical when you are a responsible leader and the conditions your organization faces are drastically different from those of the past with now "off-purpose" beliefs on which habitual actions are based. To return to the boating incident that started chapter 1, when your boat (or organization) is headed toward breakers that weren't in the inlet before, if you fail to adjust in the light of new reality, you will run it aground. With awareness of our personalities as well as our egos and ego defenses and their purposes, we are afforded a useful "crack" in our structured reality that we can peek through. It is by this process that we can change our beliefs and form values to again be "on-purpose" and we can achieve the outcome we want more rapidly.

As I navigated through that inlet, by listening to Chris and my intuition, I paid heed to what the current conditions, not my experiences and conditioning, were telling me. I watched the water and not the buoys and changed my boat's course to head out into deep water— into the unknown, uncertain of what I would find. I "built the bridge as I walked on it." By doing so, I saved my boat from potential destruction, and my passenger and me from injury. The next time I went to the inlet, another storm had hit. This time conditions were even worse, but now I didn't hesitate; I concentrated on what the water, not the buoys, was telling me. Again, we made it through safely. I was leading myself more effectively.

Expanding Awareness

If you believe your unit or team or organization would benefit by becoming more adept in expanding awareness, here are some recommendations.

1. Have your team members attend a self-awareness-based leadership development program, such as our "Leadership JumpStart®," which has been held monthly for more than twenty years. Send a leader who is held in positive regard by many; don't use the self-awareness technology as a "charm school" or place to "fix" behavioral issues. The development of real leadership and organizational adaptation is so very important for the revitalization of your company and sending someone with situation behavioral issues turns the experience in the wrong direction from the very beginning.
2. Hold facilitated feedback sessions. This needs to be done by an outside professional with lots of experience with people and business. This person can operate outside the dictates of the cultural norms and established temporary or permanent power structures to help your team and organization open up new and more effective channels of communication, feedback, and transparency in order to reduce blind spots and support better decision making, action, and behavior. Further, make the learning happen around real issues; we have found the participants retain much more as

166

most tend to be "utilitarian" and more fully value approaches that give tangible "payback" on the job.

3. Have your executive team participate in personality assessments, and make sure they are tied to the business. Many good psychologists can do this at a personal level and many experienced businesspeople are now coaching. You might also find a behavioral scientist with robust business and coaching experience to help you, especially as a regular outside member of your team.

4. Build a common language and model of leadership and self-awareness. Use systematic reinforcement. We have found that once a month is about the right frequency for a team or personal coaching event. Don't get caught up in the fad of the day or the book of the month. Consistency and repetition are really important for developing awareness. Bear in mind that memory and past beliefs are tenacious and will fight back even when they are irrational.

Chapter 8
Transforming Organizations
Changing Minds to Change Performance

> There is nothing more difficult to take in hand, more
> perilous to conduct, or more uncertain in its success
> than to take the lead in the introduction of a new or-
> der of things.
>
> —*Niccolò Machiavelli*

Certainty is not a leader's refuge, but faith coupled with strategic
action increases the probability of success when you leap from the
cliff at the edge of the quit zone through the unknown. If you combine
the qualities outlined in the Grinnell Organizational Vitality Model,
figure 2 in chapter 1, your odds of success go way up. In this chapter
we'll look at some specific points about real leadership in transforming organizations, amplifying the lessons introduced in the preceding
chapters. To start, I'll summarize the main ideas to keep in mind as
you set off on the journey into real leadership and into the transformation of your company.

Guiding Principles of Real Leadership

Here, in a nutshell, is what sets real leaders apart from those who can't or won't make the jump out of the quit zone:

- Transformation requires expanded awareness, alignment, and accountability—always in support of the mission and values, which is the organization's purpose.
- Leadership is the adaptive force of the organization. In nature, those organisms that don't change fast enough to meet the demands of the environment don't survive. The same is true of organizations. Leadership is not an external factor; it is an internal, personal commitment, one few are prepared to make. However, for a real leader who does make this commitment, there are steps he or she can take to move other leaders and followers into a state of being that will allow a change in their behavior.
- Leaders don't make certainty their purpose. Until a leader makes the jump into uncertainty, he or she is not really leading; few, if any, will follow until that leader does jump. Change, even for real leaders, is difficult, fraught with conscious and unconscious habits and ego-supporting behavior.
- Leaders lead minds. Organizations are composed of individuals working together using certain processes and following policy to achieve a common outcome. More specifically, these individuals hold a set of beliefs in varying degrees of alignment with the values and goals of the organization, and they act out of those beliefs.
- All organizational transformations come from a change of mind and perspective. Until this occurs, with the accompanying decisions, actions, and behavior that arise from those changed minds, nothing in the organization *really* changes.
- The leadership system is the network of individuals who are the "keepers of the culture" and all the perspectives,

169

behavior, judgment, and expectations therein. Transforming the organization begins with changing the perspectives, behavior, and expectations of those keepers and thus changing the culture. Once they are able to expand awareness, seek alignment, act accountably, and be on-purpose, you have a powerful leadership culture in place to balance the need for stasis.

- Leaders must change their own minds before others will change theirs. Some have to "fake it until they make it," acting behaviorally in alignment even when their passion isn't there yet. Often this requires a "leap of faith" and the ability to "stomach" many difficult decisions and actions that must be undertaken.

- There is a logic to working effectively in the human systems within the culture leaders can learn and use to create conditions and greater certainty that those who follow will change their behavior.

The Leadership Flywheel

In addition to the graphic version of the Angel Model, which is based on a pyramid, there is another way of picturing real leadership. The Vital Enterprise Model makes visible how the leader needs to integrate these characteristics within the broader context in which leaders and organizations operate in today's world. As figure 11 shows, being on-purpose and testing actions, decisions, and behavior against the mission and values of the organization are at the heart of the task of a real leader. Being aware, seeking alignment, and acting accountably all revolve around staying on-purpose. The circle radiating out from this core encompasses both leader and followers. Outside the edges of this circle are external forces—markets, customers, vendors, and society; they are beyond the circle, but they still line up with being on-purpose, and the leader has to relate purpose to them if the company is going to react with agility, adapt, and thrive.

The main point of this illustration is that each step in the leadership process, from expanding awareness to acting accountably must

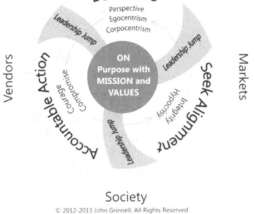

Customer

Society

Figure 11. The Vital Enterprise Model, with Purpose at the Center

be gauged against purpose and done with accountability in order to break inertia and launch purposeful momentum. That is, as others have said, purpose is the "touchstone" to determine real gold from fool's gold.

John Mackey and Raj Sisodia, in their discussion of conscious capitalism (2013), present a model that similarly contains a number of interrelated elements, all of which need to be taken into account, they argue, and treated responsibly, with respect, fairness, and consideration.

These include not only the team members (as they refer to leaders and employees) and shareholders, but also the customers, suppliers, and communities (including the environment) in which the company has a presence.

Notably, Mackey and Sisodia assert that a company must connect these elements to the higher purpose and values, not merely be concerned with short-term profit, and must make sure investors are aware of that purpose and those values.

171

Be On-Purpose

Often when companies are seeking insight into competitors, consumers, the industry, or advances in technology they create a new "position." Many books have been written about how to go about this and expert consulting firms can help organizations do it. The more difficult part of changing to adapt to new conditions, however, is transforming minds to change behavior. To make the right decisions and take aligned action to enable a company to flourish requires purpose or direction. Without it, leaders default to memory-based past decisions, past beliefs, and accustomed behavior. Defaulting to the past, to normal behavior, is not the imprint of an organization undergoing genuine transformation. Regardless of how good a new position is and all the expense of time and money it cost to determine it, these won't matter in the end if people don't decide to change.

As Covey says, "start with the end in mind"; that's the benchmark against which decisions are made and actions taken for alignment with a new desired outcome. Anyone can have all the insight in the world into competitors, consumers, and the market, but without knowing where you are going, it is difficult, if not impossible, to know which turns to take and where not to stop. Knowing your "position" isn't much help in directing you other than in telling you where you start from. A mission statement and a clear set of values tell you what "right" is, where you should head, and how you should get there. Without them, you will default to automatic habitual perspectives, insights, and behavior. With them, you have a compass and a flashlight. And remember that, as John Allison argued, having the right fundamental principles in place leads businesses to success—it is a prerequisite.

In our consulting work, Grinnell Leadership uses an organizational inquiry tool we call the VitalOrgScan™. In this process, we help the executive team develop a mission or purpose, and clarify the organization's values. We anonymously survey key leaders throughout the organization to gain their perspective on and knowledge of what "on-purpose" behavior looks like. The executive team then does an in-depth assessment of where the gaps are in perspective and behavior, as highlighted by the mission or purpose statement. This rolls into a targeted communication and leadership development process for aligning minds and behavior with the necessary future. It also serves as a great alignment tool for the executive team, to shape its members over time into a high-performing team able to expand awareness, rapidly align, and maintain accountability.

This purpose serves as a benchmark or "touchstone" for alignment and decision making in the future. One technique that is quite effective is based on a simple, but powerful, method I came across years ago while working as a consultant at a major corporation, which I believe was developed by Charles Krone; it is a technique for building an organizational mission statement or a team charter in such a way that the members know why the group exists and what they are responsible for doing. It consists of the following three phrases, which are combined and which the team comes to a rough-draft consensus to complete:

To . . . (why we do what we do)

In a way that . . . (how we go about it that differentiates us)

So that . . . (what impacts do we want to make and hopefully measure)

These phrases not only keep the mission visible, vivid, and simple, they imply how alignment should happen and they give the foundation for measuring accountability. They constitute a formula for real leadership.

Expand Awareness

Before leaders can truly expand their awareness, they must be able to maintain rationality while moving through their strong emotional defensive responses, generated by the ego's guard mechanisms, which by their nature are based in memory and defend past approaches. This is hard to do. The real leader must commit to keeping an open mind and maintain curiosity to discover how his or her behavior needs to change in order to support a future that is, at this point, only imagined, in contrast to the past and present that are concretely visible. Egocentrism and corpocentrism are powerful centrifugal forces that pull people away from the core purpose, back toward the habitual.

The first step for an organization is to expand the personal awareness of senior leaders, so that they come to see which of their own behaviors are not in alignment with the new intended outcome arising from being on-purpose. Often, very bright executives trained in the logic of administration, science, or technology think that something is wrong when approaches they created in the past are questioned. To expand their awareness usually requires input of more "truth" than they and the leaders above them are willing and able to look at or discuss. This is why an external "honest broker" often needs to get involved with the transformation process at this beginning point, building processes to properly bring information to leaders in a manner that enables them to most quickly hear it and appropriately act on it. A longtime colleague, Dr. Bill McLaurin, aptly calls this phase "building a pressure vessel," so that any defensive reactions are contained, and the individual or team can continue to align and be on-purpose.

Organizations serious about real change would be wise to send their key leaders through a self-awareness-based leadership process tied to organizational change. Seminars of this type should help build a new consciousness, the "pressure vessel" in which they can hold fast to "perspective" to gain free intelligence for obtaining insight into the self and human nature. In other words, they develop a conceptual framework within which leaders can examine behavior and thinking that the ego may not like in order to find better ways of aligning themselves and those who follow them with purpose.

Once awareness and the ability to maintain perspective begin to grow, leaders are better able to see systems, processes, attitudes, and behaviors that are "at gap," out of full alignment with the purpose of the organization. All gaps are not equally important to close; all do not offer the same leverage for transformation. Leaders who can assess the gaps clearly, once they have slipped past the ego's defenses, turn a few vital ones into objectives, and these become the focus of the effort to change the leadership system.

An example from my experience illustrates how to go about this process, and the obstacles that leaders must overcome:

The company I mentioned earlier that built hydroturbines had built those hydroturbines for many years making great profits. By the time we began to work with the company, most of the world's viable rivers had been dammed. The wise president foresaw that the market for new equipment would eventually close. He brought in a high-powered consulting firm to conduct an in-depth study of current and future market potential. The consultants determined that the renovation marketplace was where future opportunity would exist. The firm also helped the turbine company develop a "position" and "brand" that would serve it well. With this information in hand, the president realized that embracing this opportunity would bring significant changes not only in business development but also in marketing, design fabrication, and product installation. Exacerbating the problems the company faced, management had a less-than-positive relationship with unions that would likely resist the changes even though they would serve the enterprise and preserve as many jobs as possible. The consulting firm was expert at "directional-strategic" leadership, but proved unable to help with the transformation necessary to achieve the new goals tied to the new direction.

The president saw that he had to first develop among his executives awareness of the current situation the company faced and the soon-to-be urgent need to address the future successfully. He also knew that this would take quite a shift for them. When he saw the direction he needed to pursue clearly, he engaged us to perform a VitalOrgScan™; to start the process, we interviewed key personnel throughout the organization. At the same time, he sent people to our leadership program to gain insight into human nature, in how to move to a position of real leadership, and in the challenges therein.

In order to preserve the anonymity of the respondents, we edited the information gained from the interviews of key managers and supervisors, and wrote it up in brief form, then fed the results to the executives. Even though we spend a great deal of time the first day of such sessions preparing executives to hear the feedback (building the pressure vessel), it is often still difficult for them to hear information that is critical and points out shortcomings or identifies gaps between their behavior and the new direction the organization is taking. The strong ego of executives serves them well, but it does not like to be wrong and will resist new input that implies it is wrong.

After we presented the data to this group, the executives asked my partner and me to leave the room while they caucused with the president. They intended to get rid of the consultants. They saw the data as offensive and overly critical of their leadership and the organization. The president later told us that he listened to their complaints, then told them he appreciated their feedback, but that he saw us as only relaying information that people were afraid to tell the executives on the leadership team to their faces.

He further informed them that anyone who didn't feel able to accept this feedback and the necessary changes could bring their resignation letter to him on the following Monday morning and he would respect their decision. No one did. So we continued the process and over the next three years the president was able to work his way through the organization and realign it for success.

The president had made the leap, and wasn't looking back—and the others followed suit because he had. We at Grinnell refer to them as "good people with old habits." They were clearly acting "normally," But real leadership requires one to act "abnormally." Often a leader in the real leadership mode will suddenly feel like an alien, as formerly loyal employees will often treat him or her as a "stranger in a strange land."

Seek Alignment

Argue for your limitations and sure enough you have
them.
— Richard Bach, *Illusions*

Procedurally, the path from this point seems straightforward: once leaders have identified gaps and turned a critical few into specific objectives, they perform a gap analysis, examining current technical and scientific, administrative, and human processes. The processes and policies that are in alignment with the new future are left alone or reinforced. Those processes, systems, structures, and people that will not successfully address the future must be highlighted, and the executive team must agree on how to go about transforming them to support the new purpose and a successful future, recognizing that past methods may no longer allow the company to adapt with agility.

However, it's not so simple. Emotion comes into play here, and transforming organizations involves human beings. Sometimes, systems, processes, and people that are no longer in alignment are "sacred cows," cherished within the organization; and changing or eliminating processes and helping some persons move on to other opportunities will likely spark widespread resistance. At times this can be quite surprising.

Over ten years ago we were asked to develop and deliver a year-long program for high-potential younger managers—those who might one day be able to sit at the executive level. Our assignment was to initiate them into real leadership. We did two separate regional groups of fifteen managers simultaneously. As a result of the slowing economy, during the program there was a significant shift in strategy and this rather large national healthcare organization decided to capitalize on the optimization of its workforce through high-level collaboration. My team quickly went to work on what was to us and the CEO an "obviously good idea." As we held initial meetings, quite unexpectedly, one of the regional senior executives went into resistance. All his objections were addressed, but he remained adamant. He was an excellent manager-executive whom we had worked with for years, but he had some long-standing blind spots and, to us, unexpected resistance to being a more integrated part of the international organization. He worked through his resistance and is now an advocate for collaboration. But this very bright individual's first response was to resist.

At this point, to avoid as much as possible this sort of resistance, holding in-depth truth sessions among executives is important. They must fully understand the company's new direction, and they must engage in "enterprise-wide" and "future" thinking. This big challenge involves letting go of embedded thinking habits, essentially learning to think "globally" (enterprise-wide) while acting "locally" for self-referencing alignment and control. For managers trained to defend their turf and budgets against all others, such thinking is not normal. Many executives have been rewarded through the years for building and supporting an existing system. Invisible social contracts with long-term "loyal" followers often must be broken if the organization is to come into alignment with its purpose and succeed in the future.

Coming into alignment can require a very sobering and difficult series of conversations, and some executives will not get beyond the starting point, as they will feel guilty not supporting loyal followers conditioned to past approaches. The executive team must be aware of a tendency for some of its members to operate with "silent disagreement," pretending to go along with the new direction and only begrudgingly moving forward. This kind of "movement" will sabotage alignment; the sabotage is often not intentional or even conscious, but it's just as deadly as if it were. This truth raises an important guideline that you as a leader should always remember when seeking alignment:

Lack of alignment results in begrudging performance and, without accountability, it is hard to spot.

Begrudging performance creates leadership lag. It will kill a change initiative, and sometimes an entire organization. Executives who are unaware human beings would often rather continue past behavior and fail than take new action that requires some very difficult conversations and actions.

Alignment Lost

Even though begrudging performance is common on executive teams, many times alignment is nonetheless easiest at that leadership level, because it is easier to spot and directly address misalignment (if one has the courage). More difficult is the task the executive team has in gaining alignment for the new direction underneath them—one, two, and even three levels down. One of our clients is a CEO who has made a living by continually transforming his organization; he calls this group of middle managers the "crusty middle." This group has been reinforced and rewarded both financially and with position power for delivering and maintaining the wishes of executive management. They are, in essence, the stabilizing force of an organization; when stable-state management is called for, they are necessary. But when change is required, they can struggle greatly, as their habits and cultural expectations are reinforced over years of promotions and thereby deeply ingrained.

Here is a vivid example of the tremendous challenge transformation can pose and what happens when leaders do not meet it:

> Years ago we worked with a conglomerate that had taken almost a hundred years to develop to the highly profitable enterprise it was. Each of its successful companies had been selected and acquired to form a diverse yet related group of companies that always produced a successful cash flow regardless of the state of the economy. However, the CEO and several key executives figured out that they were losing to other companies a tremendous amount of work that could be kept in-house and that would provide more revenue if the work was done efficiently. In other words, if the companies in the group could cross-sell for each other, they could produce a tremendous financial bump, as well as another form of sustainability. The leadership team wholeheartedly moved forward. The team carried out the typical "cascade" rollout down and across the organizations, setting up a council to provide cross-unit communication and coordination. Everyone seemed to be on board and fully aligned.

Leadership Beyond Belief

Problems, however, surfaced fairly quickly—because self-interest raised its ugly head. The middle managers were afraid to share client leads for fear of the sister company's stealing the client. Some feared being outperformed, while others feared underperformance by their colleagues. When a unit did actually cross-sell, usually a senior middle manager would be so concerned about a "fair commission" that the client became frustrated and often left. The great opportunity the CEO and others had glimpsed slipped away, lost in the infighting.

Alignment had happened at the top, but down and across the organizations, it did not exist, nor did the trust or habit patterns to work collaboratively and in good faith with each other. Metaphorically, the "head was not connected to the body." The successful culture of a hundred years actually fought back through the mind-sets and behavior of middle management. Eventually the leadership abandoned the strategy; most of the middle managers and executives rationalized and blamed the strategy as being flawed, never realizing they had themselves done in a perfectly sound strategy that would have given them greater prosperity, security, and sustainability. Few saw it as a failure of *their* leadership, and so they learned nothing about the importance of either alignment or real leadership.

Actively Driving Alignment

One approach to achieving alignment throughout the organization, below the top levels, is to provide focused leadership development to "up-and-comers," such as the junior managers with high potential mentioned in chapter 6. Effective leadership development processes for this purpose are different from many leadership development programs we typically see in organizations today. They are targeted behavioral interventions designed to build the leadership capability of an organization using changing processes and systems as the anvil against which to forge new leadership ability and aligned cultural behavior. Creating the right psychological and social foundation for success in this endeavor is a subtle task, with little resemblance to

180

what most managers consider talent development. In carrying out this work, an organization is building for the future a base that contains rising leaders with new abilities and new behavior.

A striking example of a successful program of this sort is that of a medical supply company we worked with. When we started working with the company, it had been very successful for years, but it needed to undergo a transformation if it was to successfully compete in changing conditions with larger and in some ways more sophisticated companies in its region. Early in the process, the CEO invited me to meet his executive team. The company had never hired a leadership consultant to work with its executives before and he advised me to "go easy on them." Here's what happened:

We worked with the team for months to try to understand its "secret recipe" for success. It turned out to be its strong ethical and family values, and a savvy, "prudent" approach to risk, which later became a huge differentiator of the company from its competitors and a way to attract high-performing employees from larger companies. These deeply held values also served the company well as it prospered throughout the financial crisis and recent downturn in the economy. When we pinpointed that advantage, the executives looked at the gaps between where the company was at that point and where it needed to be when it doubled in size. They made good progress, yet the changes in behavior necessary for competitiveness were very difficult for these executives to lead in the ranks below them. They were great people with wonderful values, but had been stable-state managers for years. And they didn't seem to fully understand how important true accountability was, and they had been insulated over the years from the growing threat in the marketplace because of their strong customer commitment and long-standing positive reputation.

Fairly early in our relationship, the CEO secured help in the transformational work of a talented younger manager, who had worked his way up through a number of companies in his relatively brief career. He seemed to be a natural lead-

181

er, able to gain quick insight into problems, and to take sometimes difficult and courageous action in support of the company's mission. Once the two teamed up with their strong leadership group they decided that in order for the middle managers to shift their perspective and behavior in alignment with the enhanced vision for the company, it would be necessary to identify up-and-coming leaders. We helped them develop a customized, systematic, high-potential development process whereby a group of younger leaders who were seen as one day being capable of sitting at the executive level were brought together for one day a month for a year to learn about real leadership, and to work together on projects throughout the company.

At this first "Leadership Decathlon®," the young manager was the unofficial leader. He and fourteen others went through the process, developing insight into real leadership and building trust, as well as getting insight into the new vision firsthand from the executives who were fully aligned. Norms and expectations began to change. We taught them how to give and receive feedback to reduce blind spots, how to make decisions based on purpose, how to remain in a problem-solving mode, and how to stay on the high ground in the face of significant resistance to change. Both the CEO and the manager expected them to help the executives above them put in place the changes that were needed. In other words, the two helped the senior executives gain alignment at a level below them by going down into the organization and working with people who had not yet been totally integrated into the former culture. For those middle managers who were not in alignment above the "Decathletes," it became more difficult to maintain that position of misalignment. A few of them left to work for other companies, and only a couple left for other kinds of opportunities or retired. Meanwhile, the leadership team brought in a number of new executives who already held a similar philosophy to the one the leaders were trying to achieve. Most important, they enhanced the core values and

Transforming Organizations
"secret sauce" that had served the company for many years. Truly masterful and respectfully managed change.

The company is now much larger than it was twenty years ago. It has held a number of the high-potential development programs over that period; and each one has been different, customized to the individuals attending, as well as to the company's evolution. It is a company in alignment to its values and purpose, and it now enforces accountability much better. This experience illustrates why it is important to have in place solid accountability processes, the courage to uphold them, and the sometimes grinding work of a long-term discipline.

All Must Act Accountably

If the senior executives don't have the resolve and endurance for change, it will likely not happen. A leadership team and the organization it serves are only as strong as their weakest link, and if that weakest link is not attended to, it will slow change, creating greater risk for the enterprise and all concerned. Accountability is the set of processes that ensures that talk is translated into action and that changes in behavior, as well as other changes in the organization, take place in a timely manner. This critical step in transformation is where more failure occurs than in any other.

During a transformation, leadership must be unified. This does not mean the leadership team should not welcome feedback and divergent opinions. After consideration of relevant information and deliberation about options, however, everyone on the team has to fully support the decisions reached. Most managers will seek consensus, but this is not the goal. Instead, the senior leaders, especially the top leader, must earn their keep, using good judgment to support and make tough decisions. Once those decisions are reached, followers must, with eyes open for areas of improvement, trust their lead, following the light of the core values.

Executives and key subordinates below them must exhibit this trust by demonstrating commitment to the new direction through their behavior, especially in politically and emotionally difficult situations. For one leader to speak even occasionally behind the scenes against the team's plan, or to not hold people accountable for their new behavior, will slow the process of change, not only in that executive's area but in the whole organization. Such leaders are what I earlier termed "good people with old habits." To prevent them from disrupting the transformation, they must receive feedback when they break ranks and must be taught to stay the course, even when doing so is uncomfortable. If they can't learn how, they need to be let go quickly. One important step senior executives can take to effectively manage this process is to make sure leaders at each level have "peer teams" for regular ventilation and reinforcement. Change is emotionally difficult and it is easy to forget we are all human. Leaders need to remember that ventilation is not resistance and that many people need to voice their discomfort in the form of strong opinions before they can move on.

Organizing for Implementing Change

If you're starting an initiative to transform your organization, you need to set up a leadership team to coordinate the effort. This probably seems obvious, but perhaps less obvious is that how you do so is vital to the project's success. Excellent stable-state managers often find it difficult to provide leadership for organizational change. The questions the CEO and any other senior leaders planning such a team should ask in evaluating a potential group for this task are do they have the time, in addition to their regular duties, and can they make the tough decisions inevitably associated with changes of systems, processes, and people? If the answers tell you that the expected team of senior leaders cannot succeed at this task, you must make changes in order to establish an alternative group that can get the job done.

A common alternative is a "diagonal slice" steering committee (which we call a "stewardship team") that reports directly to the CEO and then through the CEO to the executive leadership team. This group should never be larger than twelve people; ideally it should be six to nine people, including the CEO or COO. The group's primary purpose, in addition to taking a load off the stable-state managers, is to keep tabs on all change initiatives under way in the organization. It is critically important that the CEO or COO and president be part of this team. When they are, they can provide direct support and guidance, and obtain fresh, unfiltered information about the misalignment with change happening in their organization.

Still, the team of senior executives can get this job done if the answers to the questions above are positive. This structure, in fact, can produce some side benefits as well: while the senior team is busy with the change initiatives, those managers who report to those executives must now step up and assume greater responsibilities formerly outside their domain, thus nurturing the firm's leadership potential. And a senior executive who can learn to provide both change leadership and stable-state management as needed is a much more valuable asset to the organization.

The Competitive Path Mapping tool mentioned in chapter 2 is useful for the leadership team to chart progress and make visible areas where progress is not occurring. It helps our clients logically align change actions with the strategy to achieve the new purpose and to communicate new expectations more clearly and rationally to those who are expected to change. The map becomes the record of actions taken to achieve your goals. The CEO uses this tool regularly to get updates, to create reports, and to keep track of changes. Following each year's strategic cycle, the leadership team updates the map as priorities change and projects are completed.

Accountability in Action

In chapter 3, we divided the words *accountable* and *responsible* into "account-able" and "response-able" in order to make a point that is important as you set out—you must be able to "count" or measure a goal in order to be held accountable for achieving it and you have to have the right resources to be able to attain the outcomes you're responsible for. Once your leadership team sets key objectives, then it begins negotiating the resources needed. Although such approaches as the "balanced scorecard" and "management by objectives" are useful, we still see organizations that use them fail to meet specified outcomes and time frames, thereby creating often unnecessary risk to the enterprise. The reasons they fail are familiar: a lack of courage, the persistence of old habits, and compromise.

When a company does exhibit courage, refuses to compromise out of fear, and organizes effectively to handle a challenge, the result can be a thing of beauty to behold. One example that stands out in my memory involved more than one company on a huge project to design and build an enormous office building, one of the largest such projects any of them had ever undertaken. Our team worked for three years with some real leaders from numerous organizations, private and governmental, who made everything come together:

The project was one of the last to be planned. Because this huge project was released late in the process, it was designated what people in the field call "fast track"—everything moves faster than it normally would, and every partner on the project has to work together seamlessly with verified trust in order to meet the schedule and to reduce financial risk while maintaining safety on the job. These partners were from different companies with different cultures. The lead partner knew he had a challenge in coordinating the work with various partners.

His first step was bringing together his main collaborators, from three main organizations. They all agreed on an approach known as "partnering," an intensive and rapid indoctrination into a new set of highly collaborative work behaviors and in expectation of a high level of authenticity and cooperation. To successfully accomplish this task requires tremendous leadership alignment and mutual support, as well as collaborative behavior modeled from the top.

The three leading coordinators brought together a talented technical leadership team from multiple private firms and public agencies. They quickly began building a set of shared values, as one put it, and a clear common mission. In order to ensure alignment, they designed a two-level governing structure for the project: the upper-level "principals" team and the lower-level, "boots-on-the-ground" project leadership team. Both teams focused on providing leadership and fostering open communication and mutual support, as well as operation in good faith (see appendix 4).

One way they did this was by holding regular meetings twice a month to reduce ego defense mechanisms and corpocentric parochial thinking and to focus on a vision of truly open "One-Team" communication. Members of the One-Team gradually learned to surface issues accurately and quickly, and to see problems as shared ones. They avoided blaming others. The flow of information became amazingly fast and accurate, so they were able to make decisions faster than they had initially expected. Clearly they understood the invisible human dynamics that drive the visible outcomes—and put a process in place to lead to that often unseen dimension.

About a year into the program, the primary client organization decided that the schedule needed to be shortened by six months. I was at the meeting where this decision was announced. The executives sat in stunned silence for several minutes until one team member said, "This is our challenge and we have the best chance of doing it if we work in seamless and full alignment, and belief in our success serving the mission." The team members took turns acknowledging their concerns, but also reaffirming the belief that they were in the situation together and that they would succeed together. And they did, delivering the finished building six months earlier than the original schedule.

What made this success possible was the governance process the leaders had established from the beginning, the "path forward" and a clear shared mission and set of collaborative working values that they didn't compromise on. In this simple but profound process, they wrote down agreements for performance and support, and committed to being accountable for success within the designated time. They had used this process with great discipline and had taken it very seriously. They had held themselves accountable to take on the tough challenges and to follow through in an agreed-upon time. Within this framework, they weeded out and reassigned the chronically misaligned. By the time the late scheduling challenge occurred, they were a truly aligned and accountable One-Team. (See Phelps 2012 for more on effective collaboration.)

They had not compromised on what they saw as the right things to do or on their agreements for performance, so they became a powerful leadership force throughout the life of the project. When they decided to act, they thought decisions through carefully, but once they set the direction and reached alignment, they moved forward, succeeding time and time again.

Handling Resistance

Once you have done a thorough job of translating strategy into a clear map and that map into a few key objectives, then involved key personnel down throughout the organization in communicating the changes and the expectations for new behavior, you will likely meet resistance. This is natural human behavior: we resist the new as we trust the past. Regardless of how much change makes sense, people will first view it through skeptical eyes. Jim Farr, in his excellent article "Changing Minds," points out different sources of resistance in this context: misunderstanding, fear of change, fear of failure, refusal to take executive direction seriously (often after years of empty threats and repeated change initiatives that didn't work), laziness, and incompetence. It is vital to meet resistance directly, ethically, and responsibly. Effective leadership can reduce most of the resistance arising from these causes.

People undergoing change in an organization roughly divide into three distinct conceptual categories:

- 20 percent of the workforce are "leading the leaders."
- 20 percent are stubbornly resistant.
- 60 percent are willing, but at the outset not capable of effective change because they don't yet know what you want or "how" to do it.

The early adopter-leaders are already operating with new behavior in line with the new vision and strategies. In fact, the executive team has probably gotten some of its new ideas for implementation by observing their behavior. An important point to realize is that *these people are often forgotten* because executive management is so busy putting out fires. Senior leaders need to regularly stroke them both socially and financially. Reward, recognition, and celebration are essential to fuel the long steady drive down the road of organizational change.

"It would seem that accountability when things go well would be easy," Walt Yourstone, president of VT Milcom, points out. "However, many leaders often don't take the time to recognize this desired behavior or success. Sometimes it's because they don't understand the importance of providing this feedback. Others don't want to make a special point to recognize behavior that is 'expected.' If there is a rock star on the team, they expect that person to be a rock star, so why make a special point to acknowledge their performance? In either case, the leadership misses the opportunity to reinforce desired behavior and build a culture of success."

Ironically, in fact, managers tend to give more attention to the stubbornly resistant 20 percent. Some of these people may be "loyal" to the old systems they have served for years; others may have a sense of entitlement to their jobs because they've held them for a long time (see Bardwick 1995 for an enlightening discussion of this attitude). A common error among managers undergoing the change process is to overindulge those who persist in their resistance. Compassion is wonderful and quite often useful, but when dealing with the *truly resistant*, giving helpful attention actually reinforces off-purpose behavior. Focusing on this behavior emphasizes executive attention to delinquency, inadvertently disempowering the rest of the team and reinforcing the old unwanted behavior. A much better approach is to focus on a different group.

This is the large group of people who are willing, but not yet ready. This is the "gold mine"—the group executives and their subordinates must spend most of their effort and time with. They are the solid citizens no organization can do without, and most often these are the people who will enable your organization to win a competitive advantage. Working especially with the eager, the scared, and the misinformed who can't quite yet demonstrate new behavior, you should help them to better understand what you want and give them regular feedback, both positive and, when they are off-purpose, negative. As you continue to communicate clearly the new direction, the new goals, and the new expectations, as you make clear that negative feedback is acceptable and that failure at new tasks will be tolerated as people learn, many of these will over time adopt the new desired behavior and habits, and work effectively toward the new goals.

The Critical Question: What Are the Limits of Off-Purpose Behavior?

How much time do you have to work with the incapable or the unwilling? This is a critical question the leadership team must ask itself, and it must answer it carefully but quickly. Dealing with people issues is the most difficult part of change, yet leaders must handle them well or all else is lost. The greatest risk of failure most change initiatives face comes when leaders fail to directly address in a timely and ethical manner those who are not on board with the change. To avoid this hazard, an in-depth philosophical discussion early in the process needs to happen among executives to determine the limits of tolerance that can be afforded to off-purpose behavior. You must determine whether your organization should *err on the side of working with the resistant longer or making the mistake of losing a few good people for the sake of moving the ship quickly.*

Often what is required is a balance of the obvious value of the individuals and the latitude that business constraints impose on the time line for the change; for example, turnarounds are at one extreme, since cash flow must be restored, and the time available for persuasion is tight. However, other types of change can tolerate slower action in regard to those having a difficult time. What situation are you in? One form executive resistance takes is avoiding addressing directly these tough questions.

Letting People Go

Over the many years I've worked with corporations and other organizations, I've witnessed many occasions when competent employees with good attitudes find themselves misplaced within the context of

190

new organizational strategies, yet end up in a new and often better position. I've also watched, however, as leaders wrestle with making hard, often heartbreaking choices: some loyal people will not be able to make the necessary changes in behavior in time or the organization just doesn't need their particular skills or talents going forward in its new direction. These difficult situations require a clear philosophy that the executive team supports unanimously. Each company must forge what it considers its "ethic" of how it treats not only the employees who stay but, maybe even more importantly, how it treats the ones who must leave. This is not an easy decision; financial issues often prevent management from doing what it would want to do. Amazingly, though, many executive teams and boards of directors never have this discussion early.

Creative and thoughtful solutions can be found if planning takes place early. One company I know of, for example, created a pool of outplaced employees who could be "adopted" by other areas within the firm for a certain time before they were let go. But more importantly, leaders must remember that the future "character" of the company is born by wrestling with such difficult issues in a prescribed way. Ultimately, the CEO and board of directors determine the solution, but the final decision should come only after much executive input and discussion.

Managing the Winds of Change and Organizational Turbulence

Wind is energy moving, and the strength and direction of the wind are determined by contrast—by a pressure *change*. Recently I saw the powerful effects of a change in pressure in Wrightsville Beach, North Carolina, when a high-pressure "fair-weather" system flowed into a low-pressure "stormy" system, causing gale-force winds. Similarly, the change that real leadership introduces into an organization can create stormy conditions: behavioral ones stemming from ego defense, beliefs, and old habits. But just like the blue skies that can follow a storm, a "storm" within a company can be the bellwether of a sustainable future.

Leadership Beyond Belief

When a department experiences real leadership change within a larger organization, this organizational "low-pressure system" will, as its efficiency and productivity improve, begin to pull increased energy from surrounding areas—drawing more resources and services from them. Inevitably, mistakes and negative performance feedback will increase in these areas as static operating systems, processes, and behavior cause failure to meet new demand.

If they are not enlightened, managers in the surrounding areas will sense that something is different and fear that things are going wrong. They are then likely to look for reasons outside themselves, instead of at their own ego's self-protective beliefs, the perceived need not to be wrong, or the embarrassment they feel about their performance. In short, if they don't understand what the real leader is doing or don't have self-awareness, they will blame the healthier (changing) unit. When they do, they will lose an opportunity to use the change catalyzed by the real leader as leverage to improve their own area. Executive leadership can help greatly at this point by thoughtfully "riding shotgun" on change initiatives throughout the organization, including horizontally across units.

If change is tactical or routine, or you as the leader have the luxury of time, you may experience an occasional gust of wind, or a localized thunderstorm that passes through quickly. But if the change is strategic and transformational, and requires real change, you may first have to go through a gale—or perhaps even a hurricane. The following guidelines should provide you with safe passage:

1. Remember that you are not just changing your department or area. You work within a unified system and what you do will affect those around you. Thus, you will have to educate others and help them through the process of change. When you help or hurt others in your organization, you help or hurt yourself in the long run, increasing your personal security or reducing it. The One-Team concept helps here; a smoothly functioning team requires that leaders make decisions and act in ways that go beyond their own needs and areas of responsibility. Think of a basketball player who shifts from guarding his or her

opposite when a teammate needs help guarding a star, or a football linebacker who shifts over when the play is going toward a teammate who's outnumbered by blockers. Competition between units and individuals of a unified system detracts from the team's chances of success at game time.

2. Make sure you have good metrics in place to measure your unit's results against goals that are tied to organizational mission, vision, values, and financial performance. Create a few simple charts and graphs that are easy to understand and illustrate the plan and progress.

3. Always be sure the executives in your company are in agreement with what you are improving and how you are going about it so they can support you. If those in surrounding units begin blaming you for their new errors and problems, the executives can educate them on your behalf.

4. Maintain alignment with your superior. This doesn't mean you always ask permission, but that you come with ideas for the creation or adding of value. Especially important is that there should be no surprises, good or bad. Don't go out on a limb by yourself without the support of executive leadership. If you do, you run the risk of going too fast and end up going slow; better to go slow to go fast. Take time to build relationships and support as you go.

5. Stay on the high ground. If you find yourself frustrated, don't show it; "ventilate" only to someone outside work who will keep your comments confidential. Once you descend into frustration and the "fight-or-flight" response, you are no longer leading, and you risk undoing much of what you have put into place. Train the people in your department to stay on the high ground too as they interact with people in surrounding areas, since they also have the potential to undermine the initiative.

6. Don't promise perfection or consistency. Promise perseverance. Seek feedback along the way and make course corrections as you go. You will not be able to anticipate all

the issues. To again quote Robert Quinn, you have to "build the bridge as you walk on it."

7. Get issues out in the open quickly and with the right people. Nothing goes away on its own. Agree to an issues-escalation process with your peers when problem resolution exceeds your scope of responsibility or you are at loggerheads. If you stop change, you produce regression to the mean (a return to the old, habitual system).

8. Thank people and celebrate success with those inside and outside your area. Real change can take years to achieve and the hard work of real leadership is made easier when you know that people are with you and you recognize their efforts.

9. Build self-awareness among middle and executive management. Tie this development to organizational challenges. My company, Grinnell Leadership (Chapel Hill, NC, www.grinnellleadership.com), holds a leadership seminar for this purpose every month; other companies offer similar services. Remember, too, that human behavior changes with spaced repetition over time. The one-shot quick solution many companies want doesn't exist, except as a faulty belief.

Drawing the Line

Many technical, scientific, and medical organizations have found helpful a model I introduced in 1994 and have improved over the years with input from clients, the Leadership Optimization Model. As figure 12 shows, we can conceive of leadership in companies (as well as in other organizations) as occurring on various levels, which fall on two sides of a line—above-the-line management and below-the-line leadership lines. Clients have said it helps them find the necessary balance between their human, administrative, and technical systems. If nothing else, it gives your management team, project team, or board of directors a language for seeing issues and discussing fundamental organizational and project issues with greater precision.

Level 7, goal achievement, is what you're aiming at: fulfilling your purpose. Each level going down from that point builds on previous levels; each is necessary for the organization to succeed at the level above it. Work on levels 5–7 constitutes above-the-line management: making decisions, planning, scheduling, implementing, achieving. This does not mean that you don't exercise real leadership above the line; obviously, making tough decisions and holding people accountable requires real leadership. But the language does clarify that the work above the line is the work of implementing the change initiative, in very tangible, measurable ways.

Knowing the level on which an issue falls can help provide perspective and pinpoint where effort should be directed to clear bottlenecks. For example, if your plans are too vague and not accurate, these deficiencies will limit the potential of productive level-6 work activity. If your initiative bogs down on level 6, with uncertainty, confusion, and lack of focus evident, that's probably an indication that you need to go back to level 5 and rework your plans.

Work on levels 1–4 constitutes below-the-line leadership. As we saw in chapter 4, having accurate information and having it fast is a critical element in an initiative's success or failure, which is why level 4 is also known as the "choke point," a term used by Balfour Beatty US COO John Tarpey. He calls information the "lifeblood" of an organization or project. All the decision making, planning, and scheduling on level 5 flow from accurate, timely, and useful information flow.

Levels 1–3 are where the "heavy lifting" of increasing awareness must happen. Relationships; behavior manifesting in actions, perceptions, and feelings; and mind-sets springing from beliefs and the culture are the fertile soil where real leadership can nourish the roots of success in a transformation.

If you trace the course of the arrows in the model, you discover that actions produce a cascading effect. The cascade can be negative: faulty beliefs lead to wrong perceptions and off-purpose individual behavior; which lead to poor relationships and team dynamics; which lead to bottlenecks of information flow; which reduce your ability to use good analysis and decision-making skills; which results in poor planning, subpar execution, and falling short of your goals.

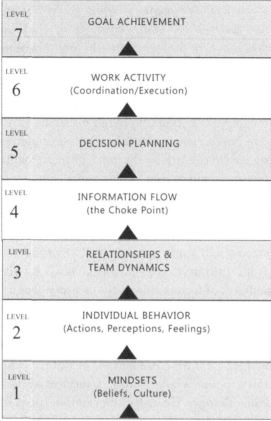

Figure 12. Leadership Optimization Model (Illustrating the Leverage of the Intangibles of Belief, Culture, and Relationships upon Organizational Performance)

Or the cascade can be positive: self-aware individuals choose useful beliefs and leaders reinforce them; people monitor ego-defense patterns and keep them in check; mutual support is the norm; information is shared, not hidden; disagreement is accepted and encouraged; the team makes decisions based on a vision of the future and rationally based on objective facts and insightful inferences; coordination and cooperation are high; and goals are achieved.

Transforming Organizations
Perseverance Is Not Overrated

Keep on keepin' on.
—Pat Dye (former head football
coach, East Carolina University
and Auburn University)

An important principle in transforming organizations is often overlooked. Even though good progress can be made quickly, most large-scale change takes three to five years to achieve. Many people leading such initiatives, however, forget the staying power needed for success, which explains why many initiatives—and some executive careers—end in the "doldrums of implementation." But as I've emphasized throughout, transformation is not easy, and it doesn't happen immediately. Realizing that you're in for the long haul and committing to that journey are essential to success. As long as you can stay on-purpose, aware of yourself and those around you, aligned with the mission and values, and holding both yourself and others accountable, you *can* succeed, and lead your organization out of the quit zone and into a prosperous future.

Some other principles are useful for your journey as well. To effectively keep track of changes, you should limit objectives to no more than five at a time. Don't make perfection your goal; success lies in thinking that "80 percent is good enough for now," with lots of ongoing tweaking, feedback, and encouragement. Identify those key people in your organization who will be affected and involve them in figuring out the tactics of change. Make sure there is continual feedback to all key leaders on their personal behavior and that of their units. Information is the Mississippi down which the organization travels; keep it flowing.

Most of all, remember that most successful change has more than occasional setbacks. One executive I know called it "fits and starts but never quits." Expect the unexpected and enjoy solving the problems that crop up—as they will. As a sign I saw in the window of a storefront church read, "Faith is the Victory." So keep it; you never know when the breakthrough will happen.

The Process of Transformation: Steps
for Organizational Success

Here is a list of steps to keep in mind while going about the work of transformation:

1. Find a better way, a difference that makes a difference—and commit!
2. Articulate the new direction; contrast it to what you have been doing.
3. Make sure your top team is clear and in true agreement with the new direction.
4. Overcommunicate the new direction, and invite your key people to help you figure out how to get there (close the gap). Make sure you involve the ones who are most affected by the changes.
5. Translate the new strategies and tactics into key objectives, overcommunicate again, and assign stakeholders in achieving the objectives. Make sure there is a top management advocate who helps the work teams succeed.
6. Stay intensely focused for eighteen months to three years. Follow up regularly; don't die in the doldrums of implementation. Hold regular "accountability meetings" to ensure that people stay focused. Use group peer-pressure reporting tactics. Embarrassment for nonperformance is a good thing: an indication that an employee is either on the verge of improvement or of being let go if no improvement is forthcoming.
7. Remember the opportunity. Make the change experience a "leadership development" experience. Tie changes to development activities for high-potential employees. See who steps up and leads quickly. They will be the ones who are smarter, or have more emotional intelligence and leadership talent, and they will be a key to your future.
8. Never get mad or show frustration when people bring problems to you.

9. Never, never, never get so busy that you forget to celebrate success!

10. Make it the norm to give feedback quickly and to coach the "good people with old habits."

11. Quickly change processes and people that aren't going to work. Since no change has unlimited time, you must err on the side of making a mistake in getting rid of a good person once in a while.

12. Communicate the vision to people three or four levels down. Build the new culture there. Align them with the direction and with senior management; middle management will follow.

13. Change is not easy work, and the senior team must support each other instead of looking elsewhere for support.

Conclusion

Purpose-driven awareness, alignment, and accountability are challenges leaders face in creating sustainable differentiation and success. To do so, many will have to leave the perceived safety of past behaviors and belief. Their other option is to cling to the same practices in a changing world—feeling safe and secure yet ignoring the changes taking place all around them. The wise know this and can listen beyond the temptation of the siren's song of past belief and instead find action in alignment with relevant purpose and values of the organizations they lead. Mastering the four elements of the angel model is their new security vessel designed for nighttime running in the open seas of inevitable change. They know, like many examples you have seen in this book, that the feared unknown is often less dangerous than the known. They can leave the past, make decisions, and take action based on what is needed to achieve further success. For the truly self-aware leader, the best predictor of future behavior is not past behavior.

The future is uncertain. Conditions are changing fast. Organizations must adapt with agility or they will enter states of entropy and erode value and perhaps eventually fail. Nonetheless, in the face of this uncertainty, it doesn't make sense for a real leader to believe in anything but success. I have learned that once you do your planning and then take the jump with real leadership it is the constant turning back and second guessing that is the basis of felt stress. A firm belief that the envisioned future will be a prosperous one, aligned with clear awareness of self and others, and of the organization's purpose and vision, enforced by insistence on accountability, enables leaders to go calmly into the unknown "building the bridge as they walk on it." In taking this step, leaders must be open and seek accurate, if sometimes ego-painful, information instead of reinforcing their blind spots. Once they gather accurate information, they can use it to plan, make tough decisions, take the leap, and work hard, while staying awake to the experience of it all.

Live Your Life

When I was young, in my mid-twenties, I was at a meeting high in the Adirondack Mountains on a cool fall day under a bright blue sky, with fallen leaves covering the path I was on. I happened to walk next to an older woman and couldn't help but notice the faded tattoos etched deeply into her skin. She, I learned, had survived the Holocaust. I was curious enough and conscious enough, though young, to ask her questions, seeking her insight into life. I did not want to rekindle her pain, so I worded my question carefully as I asked her what was the most important lesson she had learned in the concentration camp she'd been sent to. She gave me a little smile and replied, "Plan for your future, but live your life as if today was your last."

We continually live in uncertainty, whether we are advancing forward in it or not. There are no guarantees. Each morning you wake up you don't know what the day will bring. You could be bankrupt in a bull market or dead in five minutes from a building collapse. A child could become critically ill, placing all the worries about the economy in the background. You could win the lottery today. That's just how life is. If we're so fixated on winning the lottery or worried about our health or anxious about whether the strategic plan will work, we miss the opportunity to see what is in front of us *now*, in the next five minutes!

When was the last time you noticed the stars at night, a sunset or sunrise, or the smiles of your spouse and children when you came home from work? How many times have you embraced and actually enjoyed a difficult decision as a unique and meaningful experience that only you get to have? How many times have you chosen to attend to a person of lesser status without coattails for you to ride merely as a gift of attention? When did you last enjoy a day off or a vacation without revisiting work? When we don't take time to notice the world around us, and to recharge, we risk losing the joy of work—it becomes an emotional burden. Who is richer, the person who is wealthy in money and prestige, but living in the future, constantly fearful of losing that wealth, or the person who has average or little material wealth but tastes each moment of life?

Your life is a whole; the part of it in which you work cannot be separated from that whole—it's woven into the fabric. John Mackey in the introduction to *Conscious Capitalism* make this point, based on what he's learned over the decades leading Whole Foods: "I have learned that life is short and we are simply passing through here. We cannot stay. It is therefore essential that we find guides whom we can trust and who can help us discover and realize our higher purposes in life before it is too late" (2013:7).

You as a leader can choose what you believe. With the grace of having eyes held open with self-awareness you can choose to believe fully (going beyond your doubting habit) regardless of what your ego says. As one of my clients said, "I do my half and God does the other." Blind faith is dangerous; faith with eyes wide open is essential to the leader taking the jump of real leadership. With ego out of the way you will do it with awareness—find the answers and make changes in tactics as needed and stay true to the future you envision. And maybe more important you will not be so focused on the goal that you and your team will not get to "taste the experience" of transformation as you go. You can also step up and take the most difficult of actions, which is to anticipate the future, and take uncertain and sometimes unpopular action to avoid a crisis. Leaders who believe anything else will not reach their potential and provide their most effective leadership. Such a belief is not just wishful thinking; a leader who is on purpose with the organization's mission and values, who is aware of self and others and able to move beyond egocentrism and corpocentrism, who can seek alignment with the mission and values, and who can act accountably is much more likely to lead the organization successfully to a prosperous future through challenging times than a leader who lacks these learnable capabilities.

Conclusion

Maybe the biggest challenge of real leadership is learning to plan as best we can and then to walk peacefully and perhaps even joyfully, with focus, into and through an uncertain future, noticing each moment of our work and our lives as we do so. Years ago I remember John Tarpey, president of Balfour Beatty Mid-Atlantic, told a group of young leaders in a seminar we were facilitating: "Pay attention to the acquisition we are going through—it may be uncomfortable at times but there is no better time to learn. . . . Watch and learn." This is not dissimilar to what the wise woman on the path in the Adirondacks was pointing to: something that *in itself* has priceless value regardless of the circumstances we find ourselves in—living is an experience to be aware of moment by moment as we walk through our lifetimes, awakened moments one after another—many of those at work. This in my opinion is as good as life gets, regardless of how much prestige, ego satisfaction, or money we have or don't have, whether we achieve what we want or not. That is the only thing we can be certain of, but we can lose it if we forget to be aware. While it might have taken a concentration camp for some to learn that lesson, maybe others of us can learn it in the lesser crises of our times and through the glory of our successes and the learning from our perceived failures—and of those challenges and accomplishments ahead. Experience is all we get from life; leadership is one of those experiences . . . don't waste it.

And Real Leadership is one of the most meaningful experiences—if you choose it.

Appendix 1
Organizational Integrity: The Ethics of Working Together

Most people know right from wrong, whether it is telling the truth, following the Golden Rule, not cheating in sports, or playing it straight on our personal tax returns. But while personal integrity is fairly straightforward and understood, *organizational integrity* is less clear and almost never discussed.

At the most superficial level, organizations are people working together to achieve a common outcome or goal that would be more difficult or impossible to do alone. At the purest level of analysis it is the values and beliefs of employees that drive behavior that creates outcomes. The degree of alignment within that psychosocial and conceptual framework is the basis of the effectiveness of an organization. Whether the organization is a two-person team, a member of the Fortune 100, a government agency, or a sports team, the ethics of working together apply. People who work in organizations often don't recognize the agreements they made when they decided to join the organization. By joining, they adopt a set of overt or tacit "working agreements." The problem is that when these agreements go unnoticed and undiscussed, unstated rules may come to govern organizational behavior, thereby creating unintended negative consequences. Unstated rules could not only prove embarrassing but also result in wasted time, resources, and financial strength. As an example, few talk about *vertical and horizontal teamwork* and communication during the hiring process. All of this often results in "good people with old habits" inappropriately leading, following, and communicating. Coordination then becomes awkward, which dampens the organization's power of execution. *Organizational integrity* is present when the people within the organization openly discuss and adopt ethical strategies, as well as clearly articulate and expect ethical standards of behavior in order to achieve desired outcomes together.

Organizational Integrity Principles

Grinnell Leadership recommends that the members of an organization aspiring to have organizational integrity begin by agreeing to the following:

1. It is leadership's responsibility to provide a clear ethical direction for the organization, a direction that is well thought out and viable for the organization's purpose. The leaders must also clearly articulate this direction, ensure that followers understand it, and create implementation plans; they must make sure, as well, that followers understand the purpose and that the organization's values are clear to them. As a part of establishing this ethical direction, the leadership must ensure an environment where there is an opportunity to create, grow, and develop, one where self-expression, responsibility, integrity, respect, diversity, and service to the greater good are not only encouraged but strongly reinforced.

2. It is the employee's responsibility to work diligently to understand the direction and the implementation plans, and to ask for further clarification if they are not clear. The employee is responsible for grasping the organization's purpose and being clear on its values. And it is also the employee's responsibility to provide feedback and input on the direction and plans to ensure that the direction chosen truly reflects the best the organization can be. Ultimately, however, those who wish to remain within the organization must be self-motivated in aligning their attitude and behavior with the chosen direction. We call this "being on-purpose."

3. If an employee continues to be "off-purpose," it is leadership's responsibility, in service to the enterprise, to remove the employee. This does not apply to initial "fear-based change resistance" or situational "burnout," where coaching or psychological or health counseling may prove helpful.

4. Leadership and the employees are mutually responsible to provide open and honest feedback, work-related transparency, and input on the progress of the implementation, so that this effort continues to be viable and makes a real difference in behavior, instead of being just another nice plaque in the lobby.

Appendix 2
Levels of Leadership (Not Management) Development

Leadership is the adaptive force of an organization. Without leadership, organizations enter states of "slow death" or entropy (Quinn 1993). Leadership *is not* management and the two should not be confused. Although important, management skills and techniques are mechanistic and much easier to monitor, master, and perform. It is usually the lack of leadership that frustrates the achievement of organizational breakthrough—and leadership needs a separate set of targets and path of development from management.

Focus of the Chart Below: Low, Moderate, and High relate to the emphasis of development, *not* the importance of the activity. Ideally, an organization develops leadership adeptness sequentially, with earlier development as foundational for the "next level" of responsibility. The organization can carry out remedial development, but it should be less necessary, as those who are incapable will be found earlier if there are clearer expectations and definition of leadership than previously.

	Directional/ Thought	Organizational	Interpersonal	Technical/ Scientific Administrative
CEO/President	Moderate	Low	Low	Low
Executive	High	Moderate	Low	Low
Manager	Low	High	Moderate	Low
Supervisor	Low	Low	High	Moderate
Professional/ Associate	Low	Low	Low	High

Levels of Leadership
Definitions

Directional Leadership: Continually clarifies, lives, and demonstrates the values of the organization. Ensures that the desired outcome (financial and otherwise) and the path to success are clearly measured and understood by the organization. Provides processes for strategic thought leadership as needed. Easily grasps high-level (market outside-in) thinking. Clearly understands and can articulate the service or product, target customers, and market well. Succinctly explains the firm's competitive edge. Sees industry habits, blind spots, and weaknesses as areas that can be exploited for competitive advantage and differentiation. Has demonstrated in tough situations the ability to align disparate agendas and hold people accountable to clear metrics. Sees the abstraction of organizational culture and can lead executive management to shape it for success. Understands and always considers the organization's contributions to and potential impact on society.

Example: CEO and president would have received developmental experiences as executive managers and learned through performing the strategic planning processes over a number of years. They now facilitate and mentor the executives to perform the process well. The managers would be less involved in the strategic planning; they might provide input, but would not drive the process or make the final determination of direction. The managers led by the executives would, instead, work to take the strategic plan and identify issues, gaps, and barriers, and build an execution plan (organizational leadership). Managers would be guided to develop clear metrics, clarify outcomes, and hold response-able discussions, as well as hold accountability. Managers reporting to the CEO and president would be accountable to deliver those results with the support of the executives. Consultants and trainers can be used for just-in-time advice and just the right amount of learning to "help," but not "do," the work for the executives and managers.

Development Experience: Business school executive education, Young Presidents Organization, Vistage, executive development program. Participate on boards of directors and industry think tanks.

Organizational Leadership: Works "on the business, not in the business." From the strategic plan, facilitates the development of a coherent targeted execution plan (behavioral, cultural, and business). Efficiently coordinates organizational resources for the execution of the plan to achieve tangible changes, as well as intangible ones, such as organizational responsiveness, leadership, and accountability. Can build accountability "touchpoint" systems and ensures discipline for these management processes. Leads those who lead others. Can lead significant changes in systems and behavior within the five operating systems: financial, technical, administrative, human, and market. Builds effective execution plans and has the ability to lead in difficult changes of organizational behavior at optimal speed. Is optimistic (but not blindly so) and sees change as an anvil of opportunity to forge a superior leadership system. Looks to the future and builds infrastructure to support a larger business.

> **Example:** Executives and select mangers would receive development in the creation of effective business plans, as well as in the establishment of accountability processes. With the input of supervisors, identify specific processes, people, and technologies that are out of alignment with the strategic direction of the organization. Once these are understood, they would focus on the highest leveraging changes (Pareto principle 20/80 rule). They would help the supervisors set up action plans and projects, and would hold them accountable (with support and training) for results. As an initiative of their leadership, the president and executives would lead a yearly Talent Mapping process for the strategic development of high-potential younger leaders. Balanced scorecard for change initiatives must be developed. (Grinnell Leadership has a template, if one is needed.)

Levels of Leadership

Development Experience: Self-awareness-based leadership development program (if leaders have not attended systematic, high-potential development program), strategic planning processes, execution planning process (similar to my company's VitalOrgScan™), mentor for high-potential development program, personal leadership coaching, manage acquisitions, run multiple areas of the business.

Interpersonal Leadership: Supervisors are first tasked with leading and creating results through the effort of others. Managers are similar and have to lead others who lead others. Someone adept here understands task and relationship leadership behavior and how to optimize the two. The effective leader can build and lead teams, both project and management. At the management level, focuses on building leadership around him or her to leverage others' time and energy. Learns to see problems as opportunities for all types of people development, both technical and human. Can work collaboratively and lead effectively with a wide variety of personalities, motivations, and cultures. Knows how to read people, and can readily align the motivations of others with their goals and the goals of the organization. Sees feedback as necessary for high performance. Can deliver feedback in a timely, respectful, effective, and honest manner. Is not fearful of ego defense or emotional response. Deeply understands that, in helping or hurting others' performance or reputation within their organization, leaders help and hurt the larger organization—and ultimately themselves.

> **Example:** Supervisors are usually selected from the high-performing technical ranks of professionals and associates. This indicates necessary drive for the requirements of leadership, but not the skill or nerve for it. They are often technical experts who demonstrate a tendency toward higher emotional intelligence. However, this is not enough, and they would need to be given a solid model and language of motivation, influence, and leadership. They would also need to learn how to give and receive feedback, and more importantly, how to use that information as a basis for improvement. At the man-

ager level, there are often suboptimal siloing effects. The manager would be developed and involved in processes to optimize the "corpocentric*'" boundaries between departments and divisions in order to open up the free flow of information to improve organizational communication, support, and performance.

Developmental Experience: Basics of supervision, communications training, performance feedback training, 360 multi-rater, difficult discussions training, self-awareness-based leadership development, Six Sigma black belt.

Technical/Administrative/Scientific Abilities: Is an "expert" in his or her field, whether medical, technical, scientific, administrative, or other. Always seeks to be the best. Follows standard procedures, but is always looking for more effective ways to deliver better customer service. Looks to align own behavior with the values, missions, and strategic business plan of the organization. Is a leader in all he or she does, looking for ways to help and work with others most effectively in serving the mission. Understands process improvement and perhaps is involved in Six Sigma and other structured approaches to systematic improvement and problem solving.

> **Example:** For the purpose of customer satisfaction, a branch manager seeks out bank policy and becomes more proficient in the most effective, economical, and safe technology and practice for lending. An administrative assistant seeks to quickly understand and align his or her processes with the bank's most recent management accounting and balanced scorecard system in order to help improve the use of management's time. Tellers encourage their branch manager to hold an alignment session to encourage the teamwork and brand management of a local branch. With Six Sigma processes, associates in the retail loan area of the bank make a significant reduction in overhead and understand how this contribution affects the bank's competitiveness.

Developmental Experience: Six Sigma yellow belt, green belt, team coaching alignment process, self-awareness-based leadership development program.

*Corpocentrism: A term I coined in 1994 to describe the organizational phenomenon similar to egocentrism and ethnocentrism. Without corpocentrism, human beings cannot benefit from the advantages of a team. With too much corpocentrism, information flow is blocked, interpersonal support is limited to "insiders," and the organization suffers in its agility and performance. The goal of management is to "optimize" corpocentrism.

Appendix 3
A Guide to Meditation

We regularly use this process, based on guidelines from Borysenko (1987), in some of our workshops to help participants learn to become more mindful and reduce stress and over time manage their minds better. We find it a useful tool, in conjunction with other techniques, for people to gain awareness in their lives. Following this process will aid you in becoming more mindful and less controlled by anxiety and fear.

The first step is to find a location where you can concentrate, without interruption from other people. Find a place away from activity and use the same place each time—and don't use it for anything else. As you keep using it for this purpose, your mind will associate it with meditation. Let others know not to bother you and put away your cell phone. As Borysenko colorfully puts it, "Do not disturb unless there is blood involved." Make sure you are comfortable, cross-legged on the floor, if you prefer, or sitting up straight in a chair.

As you begin, close your eyes. Relax. One method for accomplishing this is to focus on each part of your body, starting with your head and working your way down to your feet, breathing in deeply, then releasing the tension as you breathe out. Focus on your breaths, in and out. This helps increase awareness—mindfulness. Don't exaggerate your breathing; just be aware of it.

As you practice mindfulness in this way, your mind will wander away from your breathing and start thinking. This is normal. You will likely become anxious, perhaps frustrated, when your mind strays and you begin thinking the many inconsequential thoughts, the empty mental chatter, that fill our minds every day. This is normal. You may worry that you're not practicing meditation correctly. This too is normal.

The key is how you respond. When you notice yourself worrying about whether you're being properly mindful, tell yourself you are judging, accept that you're doing it, and focus on your breathing again. Similarly, if you notice that you're thinking, acknowledge that you are and go back to noticing your breathing. As your mind relaxes, pay attention to your surroundings; just notice what you're hearing, being in the moment. This is being aware.

You will continue to become distracted each time you meditate. When you do, don't worry; your mind will be aware for only short intervals. But those intervals are valuable, making you mindful. And you can improve your ability to return to awareness as you find thoughts distracting you. Borysenko quotes St. Francis of Assisi, an experienced meditator: "You can't stop the birds from flying back and forth over your head, but you can stop them from nesting in your hair." So when you find yourself distracted, bring yourself back to your breathing, and notice what you hear and feel and smell.

It's helpful to meditate regularly, ten to twenty minutes each day. Don't set any expectations for yourself other than sitting down to do it. When you find yourself judging yourself for failing to be mindful, tell yourself matter-of-factly that you're judging, then breathe in, breathe out. Keep breathing, in and out, noticing your breaths, relaxing your body. I tend to be more action oriented and use it throughout the day as I am "noticing the doing."

You'll find that, as you practice mindfulness, you do relax for several moments each time. When you relax in this way, you're releasing tension and letting go of the anxiety that your ordinary thoughts bring. You're exercising your conscious mind and you'll find that you can carry over these techniques into your everyday living, becoming aware, breathing in and out, recognizing that you're thinking in a certain pattern, and finding relaxation in the midst of the activities that cause you stress.

One thing to be aware of is that when you begin practicing meditation as described here, you're likely to find yourself becoming sleepy. You do so because your body is accustomed to going to sleep when you close your eyes. This is why you want to sit with your back straight and why you want to sit rather than lie down. As you continue to practice mindfulness, you'll be less likely to drift off into sleep.

Borysenko points out that it's easy to be distracted by all the tasks we have to do, as thoughts of them pop into the mind, but that this is natural because we're not focusing on work, which can block them. You should not become frustrated when those thoughts pop up. You're not meditating poorly. Notice when you're thinking such thoughts and go back to noticing your breathing, and becoming aware. "The primary goal of meditation is not relaxation," she says. "It's awareness. . . . Relaxation is a side effect of learning how to meditate." When you notice that you are thinking and can let the thoughts go without judging yourself, you are gaining awareness. In regard to this process, Borysenko uses a vivid analogy: it is similar to "trying to balance your checkbook with the television turned on."

Appendix 4
The Big Ten Collaborative
Leadership Behaviors

The behaviors below are demonstrated by the best collaborative organizations and are typically a part of their culture. They are not inclusive of all effective behaviors. Note that there is nothing mentioned about comfort or the lack of challenge.

Success Behaviors

1. *Communicate Openly, Accurately, and Quickly:* Contrary to popular belief, tough feedback and issues between colleagues openly handled build team strength. Sharing the "brutal facts" (Collins 2001) in a non-brutal way is good for teams. *Nothing goes away on its own.* Inter-organizational process issues, as well as interpersonal problems, are made worse when not brought up soon enough within the team. If you hide one, hold back, and take the "sucker's choice" for short-term comfort you *later* pay the longer-term price of higher risk to the enterprise. Don't punish the messengers; they are probably *real* friends.

2. *Lead Strong:* All organizations have crises. The worse these storms, the stronger the leadership and courage required—feel the gut tighten and act well. The best organizations come together in crisis. Poorly led organizations look for the escape hatch of *blame, self-service, finger pointing, political maneuvering, and self-protection.* Fight, flight, or freeze is not going to make things better! Use your neocortex (thinking part of the brain) instead.

3. *Trust, Verify, and Urgently Solve Problems:* The sooner you can spot a problem the better. Trust is essential for success, but verification helps find blind spots and issues *early.* Issues that aren't recognized or communicated early are surprising and often look daunting, but probably aren't—especially if you involve those people who are affected by the problem. They've had lots of experience you

215

don't know about. Use their knowledge and yours; then quickly solve it within the team at the lowest levels. However, after your team has given it your best shot and still can't figure it out, escalate issues openly with an issues *escalation process* and expect quick response from your executives.

4. *Decide with the Purpose in Mind:* Collaboration requires the right people at the table to make the decision. Sometimes one person. Regard-less, "*Being On-Purpose* is 'why' you are here." Be *on-purpose* by keeping what's best for the larger enterprise and values in the forefront of your thinking and decision making. Don't let self-interest or departmental or divisional interest or fear-based politics drive decisions.

5. *Recognize Vulnerability:* Everything you do either helps or hurts your coworkers in your department and partner departments. Helping your partner be successful is "enlightened *other* interest." Conversely, hurting a partner will only take money or reputation out of your pocket in the long run and ultimately degrades the organization's brand, which erodes enterprise sustainability. Team members need each other to meet the organizational purpose, and aren't completely in charge of their own destiny—*you are vulnerable to your teammates' performance. The open flow of information is everyone's life preserver.* If you block the flow of information, you raise the *risk* for all. Make decisions and promises thoughtfully and keep the ones you make—thereby building trust in yours and your department's performance. Trust but also make sure you verify. We all make mistakes. When you realize you have messed up, do the right thing and let others know right away. Most problems when found early can be creatively corrected.

6. *Know When to Lead and Follow:* You may be leading today but following tomorrow. Know the business plan, including *leadership handoffs*. It's about getting the job done—not who's in charge.

7. *Keep the Transformation Moving:* You can sort blame out later if need be. To keep things moving may require help from a higher authority when goals of team members are misunderstood, misaligned, and in a logjam. It is important to document well so you can go back later to do lessons learned and to sort things out if need be.

The Big Ten Collaborative Leadership Behaviors

8. *Forgive (Self and Others); It's Practical:* Learn the lesson and take action. Let go of the *embarrassment* (shame) and move forward—fast. Instead of continuing to worry about having had a better past, find ways to creatively recover the cost or time with great performance in the future.

9. *Find Opportunity:* While the team is busy, make time to look ahead and find ways to work more efficiently and collaboratively to enhance service, sell more, and save time, effort, material, and money.

10. *Show Appreciation:* Catch people "doing it right." If you see on-purpose behavior, thank them. Organizational change projects are often long and hard. Thank those in surrounding departments who made your life easier. Interim recognition for a job well done enhances endurance and motivation, which pays great dividends for all.

Appendix 5
Delegation: The Art
of Letting Go (Properly)

A rite of passage from being a manager to becoming a leader is the practice of delegation—a topic that has come up in most of my leadership workshops and coaching over the past twenty-five years. My good fortune is having worked with many savvy executives who have successfully made it through this emotionally challenging fire. Although it was never easy, they found a way to let go of the past to be able to ascend to a broader role in which they could further leverage their talents. Many learned the hard way, butting their heads against divorce, alienated children, burnout, and, for some, repeated failure. Yet they eventually mastered it and learned how to avoid many of its traps. Here are a few tips I've picked up over the years based on what I call "managing at the waterline" (see figure 13).

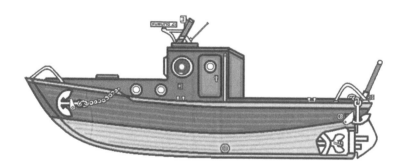

Figure 13. "Managing at the Waterline"

Delegation

The Purpose of Delegation

The fundamental purpose of delegation is to give yourself a "time payment." With this time payment you can attend to those nontechnical or nonadministrative issues that are related to your job. You can look ahead and address systems and process design, and policy deployment, as well issues and opportunities such as morale and the development of your people. This is all done to build a human infrastructure that can "handle the weight" of execution with a minimum of necessary attention from you.

Key Elements

The old saying "You can't make a silk purse out of a sow's ear" is fitting, since the character of the person you are delegating to will be a limiting factor in your successfully getting a time payment. In reality, delegation has as much to do with the delegate as it does with you, the leader. If a follower doesn't have the requisite drive, ambition, or ethic of personal accountability, you can do little to increase your scope in a sustainable way. These underpotentiated types will, at best, give you only partial support. Make your assessment early and determine if the real issue is one of character, confidence, or knowledge. The latter two can be developed, with time; if there is concern about character, however, back up the role with other followers and seek the help of your human resources. But whatever you do . . . punt as quickly as you can.

Letting Go—Properly

Some work activities for which you are responsible happen "below the waterline" and will "sink the ship" if not done right. These are the items either not meant to be delegated or meant to be delegated only to the most competent, caring, and trusted few. The vast majority of assignments and issues that arise, though, are "above the waterline."

Making the distinction between the two is the first step to successful delegation. Many technically, scientifically, or administratively trained people don't do this; instead, all assignments are linked in their minds. This blind spot is often due to their egos' being addicted to perfection or the "need to be needed"—yoking them to the behavior that made them successful in the past, but that will limit their potential for leadership going forward.

Above-the-waterline assignments, if not done with the expected level of quality or timeliness, are the savvy leader's classroom. These leaders highlight errors and respectfully take their followers through a learning experience. However, many managers (for the rationalized reason of efficiency) fall into the trap of telling their followers what to do. This just reinforces the manager's ego, bolstering his or her sense of relevance or intelligence, but reducing the follower's confidence. Instead, a much better approach is to ask the follower to come up with the solutions. If there is a time constraint or a huge knowledge gap the delegate can always be told to talk with someone who has dealt with a similar situation in the past. This "kills three birds with one stone": the manager does not have to take time to explain or teach, he or she demonstrates confidence in the employee being consulted, and people learn to reference each other instead of the manager, which adds to the latter's time payment.

Sometimes you will have to step in, but this should be a last resort. This approach is based upon the old Harvard Business School prescription that "managers should appropriately disallow employees from putting problems (monkeys) on the managers back"; or as Susie Greene, a colleague, often says, "Only monkeys with bananas." That is, establish the expectation that if they feel they must bring a problem to you, they must also bring their best solution. Always let them know you appreciated their bringing up an issue (don't ever show frustration when they come to you), but remind them of the longer-term goal of solving problems and assuming responsibility at the lowest possible level, and escalating appropriately. Most important, thank them for preventing you from being surprised by an issue after the fact.

Delegation

Reporting Is *Not* Micromanagement

To get a really great time payment, your goal should be to systematically and carefully move items from below the waterline to others to handle. This is a risky move in the short term, yet it's often more risky for your career and for the company in the long run if you don't. There are some simple guidelines that must be followed with discipline to reduce below-the-waterline risk.

1. Pick a person who is ready or close to ready to take on the challenge. It stretches that person (and you) out of your comfort zones, but isn't in the "terror zone."
2. Delegate in three stages. The first stage is "close reporting," whereby you may ask those you have chosen for this responsibility to report frequently, perhaps even daily. Let them know that micromanagement is not your intention, but rather that frequent reports enable you to be kept aware of things in your area of responsibility. As they demonstrate competence with this newly delegated task, gradually extend your expectation for reporting to increasingly longer intervals, such as weekly or bimonthly. The goal is to fully delegate with an agreement that if it appears that something will go wrong, they will let you know early.
3. Always let them know you want *"no surprises, good or bad."* And that you expect them to report to you at a specific time and place. *Always ask them to come to you!* If they don't come on time, don't chase them down, but let them know that if they do not appear at the prescribed time and with the report you have asked for, it will be difficult, if not impossible, for you to delegate additional responsibility to them. *Do not* let even a small infraction go by without addressing it. Most of the time this will result in a shift in their behavior. If not, you have a bigger problem, as this demonstrates lack of drive, caring, and an ethic of personal accountability.

221

Leadership Beyond Belief

4. Always have what Tim Gelbar, the former president of AMEC Power and Process Americas, calls "touchpoints." That is, think through a *few* key places in your unit or organization where you will notice when things are *beginning* not to go well. Most important is that you need to be disciplined about keeping track. At a high level, effective leaders know what is happening in their organizations.

Comfort Means You Aren't Delegating

Last, if you aren't uncomfortable delegating, you probably aren't really doing it and are not going to get the future time payment you desire. When you follow the guidelines above you should still feel a bit anxious, if you are really making progress. If not, you are probably talking a good game and delivering little. A year later there will be no appreciable difference in your performance; you will still be doing what you are doing now, and both you and the organization are likely to suffer. However, if you practice the guidelines above, a year from now you will have freed up significant amounts of time to use as you choose, either personally or professionally.

> Courage is not the absence of fear; it is not letting our fear control us.
> —Rolling Thunder to Billy Jack (from the movie *Billy Jack*, 1971

References

Bardwick, Judith M. 1995. *Danger in the Comfort Zone: From Boardroom to Mailroom—How to Break the Entitlement Habit That's Killing American Business*. 2nd. ed. New York: Amacom.

Borysenko, Joan. 1987. *Minding the Body, Minding the Mind*. Reading, MA: Addison-Wesley.

"Clerical Staff Bears Brunt of US Jobs Crisis." 2013. *Financial Times*, April 2, p. 1.

Collins, Jim. 2001. *Good to Great: Why Some Companies Make the Leap . . . and Others Don't*. New York: Harper Business.

Deutsch, Clay, and Andy West. 2010. *A New Generation of M & A: A McKinsey Perspective on the Opportunities and Challenges*. New York: McKinsey.

Farr, James N. "Changing Minds." 1994. *Executive Excellence*.

———. 1998. *Supra-conscious Leadership*. Huntington, WV: Humanomics.

Farr, James N., and John R. Grinnell. 1994. "The Art of Causing Followership." *Business Leader*.

———. 2009. "Executive Amplitude." Grinnell Leadership, Chapel Hill, NC.

Goleman, Daniel. 1995. *Emotional Intelligence: Why It Can Matter More than IQ*. New York: Bantam.

Gonzalez, Maria. 2012. *Mindful Leadership: The 9 Ways to Self-Awareness, Transforming Yourself, and Inspiring Others*. Mississauga, ON: Wiley.

Grinnell, John R. 2010. "Agility: The Seventh Sigma." Grinnell Leadership, Chapel Hill, NC.

———. 2012. "One-Team." Grinnell Leadership, Chapel Hill, NC.

Jackson, Phil, and Hugh Delehanty. 1995. *Sacred Hoops: Spiritual Lessons of a Hardwood Warrior*. New York: Hyperion.

"John Allison." 2011. *Business Leader*, May–June. 39.

Keirsey, David, and Marilyn Bates. 1978. *Please Understand Me: Character and Temperament Types*. Del Mar, CA: Prometheus.

Krzyzewski, Mike, with Jamie K. Spatola. 2009. *The Gold Standard: Building a World-Class Team*. New York: Business Plus.

Lencioni, Patrick. 2002. *Five Dysfunctions of a Team: A Leadership Fable*. San Francisco: Jossey-Bass.

———. 2012. *The Advantage: Why Organizational Health Trumps Everything Else in Business*. San Francisco: Jossey-Bass.

Leonard, George. 1991. *Mastery: The Keys to Success and Long-Term Fulfillment*. New York: Dutton.

Mackey, John, and Raj Sisodia. 2013. *Conscious Capitalism: Liberating the Heroic Spirit of Business*. Boston: Harvard Business Review Press.

Peters, Thomas J., and Robert H. Waterman, Jr. 1982. *In Search of Excellence: Lessons from America's Best-Run Companies*. New York: HarperCollins.

Peters, Tom. 2013. "Human Creativity Is the Ultimate Economic Resource." TEDx. Manchester, VT, June 22. Available at http://www.tompeters.com/slides/special.php.

Phelps, Andreas Floros. 2012. *The Collective Potential: A Holistic Approach to Managing Information Flow in Collaborative Design and Construction Environments*. San Francisco: Turning Point Press.

Quinn, Robert. 1996. *Deep Change: Discovering the Leader Within*. San Francisco: Jossey-Bass.

———. 2004. *Building the Bridge as You Walk on It: A Guide for Leading Change*. San Francisco: Jossey-Bass.

Sanvido, Victor, and Mark Konchar. 1999. *Selecting Project Delivery Systems: Comparing Design-Build, Design-Bid-Build, Construction Management at Risk*. State College, PA: Project Delivery Institute.

Senge, Peter M. 1990. *The Fifth Discipline: The Art and Practice of the Learning Organization*. New York: Doubleday Currency.

———. 2009. *The Power of Presence*. 2 CDs. Sounds True.

Tavris, Carol, and Elliot Aronson. 2007. *Mistakes Were Made (but Not by Me): Why We Justify Foolish Beliefs, Bad Decisions, and Hurtful Acts*. Orlando, FL: Harcourt.